BLENDER 4.2
User Guide

For Beginners and Professionals

A Complete User Guide to Enhanced Animation, Rendering, and Sculpting for Seamless Production for both Beginners and Professionals.

Joy Joseph

Table of Contents

INTRODUCTION

You can use Blender to generate 3D visualizations, including VFX shots, 3D animations, and still photos. Video editing is also possible. Because of its fast development approach and unified pipeline, it is ideal for individuals and small studios.

Blender is a cross-platform program that works with Windows, Linux, and macOS. In comparison to other 3D creative programs, it also requires comparatively less memory and disk space. To ensure a uniform user experience on all supported hardware and platforms, its interface makes advantage of OpenGL.

Blender is a versatile tool that can be used for nearly any type of media production. It is used by professionals, enthusiasts, and companies worldwide to produce motion graphics, TV series, concept art, storyboarding, feature films, gaming components, and animations.

Blender may be used for a multitude of projects, but learning the fundamentals could be intimidating at first. However, with a few hours of work and the appropriate study materials, it is feasible to get comfortable with Blender.

Though primarily intended as a reference, this handbook is a nice place to start. Additionally, there are a ton of online video tutorials available from niche websites.

Blender is still only a tool, despite its infinite capabilities. Great artists study and practice disciplines like human anatomy, composition, lighting, animation principles, etc. before they can produce masterpieces with brushes or buttons.

There is additional technical intricacy and language related to the underlying technology in 3D creating applications like Blender. The vocabulary of the digital artist includes terms like UV maps, materials, shaders, models, and "subdivs." By knowing these terms, even in general, you can make the most out of Blender.

You too may become a great artist if you continue to study this tutorial, discover what a fantastic tool Blender is, and have an open mind about new artistic and technological endeavors.

Key Features
- Blender 4.2 expands the functionality of the program and offers a number of new features and enhancements to improve user experience. Among the important points to note are:
- Better User Interface: You can now explore and arrange your workspace more easily thanks to improved usability and customization options in the interface.
- Improved Sculpting Tools: Artists can now effortlessly construct intricate models with more control and accuracy thanks to new brushes and sculpting features.
- Advanced Animation Features: New keyframing capabilities, enhanced graph editor capability, and more

user-friendly rigging and posing controls have been added to the animation tools.

- Real-Time Rendering with Eevee and Cycles: Blender's potent rendering engines, Eevee and Cycles, are still being updated to provide lifelike results and real-time rendering capabilities.
- Geometry Nodes: With additional development, the Geometry Nodes system now offers greater power and flexibility for generative modeling and animation.
- Asset Browser: By managing and categorizing assets, the new Asset Browser facilitates the reuse and sharing of resources between projects, thereby streamlining the process.

CHAPTER 1: Getting Started
⊥ Installing Blender 4.2
➢ Installing On Windows

It is simple to install Blender on a Windows computer. This is a comprehensive tutorial that will assist you with installing Blender 4.2 on your PC.

STEP 1: Download Blender

- Go to the Blender website: Visit Blender's official website.
- Open the Downloads Page by clicking here. You may access the download page by clicking the "Download" button.
- Choose the Windows Version: Windows 32-bit and 64-bit versions may both use Blender. To benefit from greater RAM and for improved performance, the 64-bit version is advised. To get the installer, click the relevant link.

STEP 2: Run the Installer

- Find the Downloaded File: After the download is finished, locate the Blender installation file (typically called blender-4.2.0-windows-x64.msi or something similar) in your Downloads folder.
- Launch the Installer: To start the installation procedure, double-click the installer file.

STEP 3: Install Blender 4.2

- Pay attention to the Setup Wizard: It will lead you through the installation procedure. Press "Next" to proceed.

- Select Installation Location: You have the option to enter a new location or use the installation directory that is used by default. Press "Next" to continue.
- Choose Components: You have the option to add shortcuts and "Blender Player" as extra components. Usually, it's acceptable to keep the default settings chosen. Press "Next."
- Install: To start the installation, click the "Install" button. The installer will install Blender on your computer by copying files. This might need many minutes.
- Complete Installation: Click "Finish" to close the Setup Wizard when the installation is finished. It could possibly be possible for you to start Blender right now.

STEP 4: Launch Blender

- Upon installation, you may locate the Blender shortcut by looking for "Blender" in the Windows search box or by going to your Start Menu.
- Start Blender: To start the program, click the Blender icon. You can be asked to choose your desired keymap (Blender's default, industry standard, etc.) when you first use Blender.

STEP 5: Check the Installation

- Upon installation, you may locate the Blender shortcut by looking for "Blender" in the Windows search box or by going to your Start Menu.
- Start Blender: To start the program, click the Blender icon. You can be asked to choose your desired keymap (Blender's default, industry standard, etc.) when you first use Blender.

Troubleshooting

- Installation issues: Verify that you have the required permissions and that your system satisfies Blender 4.2's minimal requirements if you have installation issues.
- Blender could need certain Microsoft Visual C++ Redistributables if they are missing. Permit the installer to download and install these components if requested.
- Graphics Drivers: To prevent graphical glitches or performance problems, make sure your graphics drivers are up to date.

➢ System Requirement For Windows

	Recommended	Minimum
OS	Windows 10/ Windows 11	Windows 8.1 (64-bit)
CPU	8 cores	4 cores that Support SSE4.2
RAM	32 GB	8GB
GPU	8 GB VRAM	2GB VRAM with OpenGL 4.3

➢ Installing on macOS

STEP 1: Download Blender 4.2

- Go to the Blender website: Go to Blender's official website.
- Visit the page for downloads: To get to the download page, click the "Download" button.
- Choose the macOS Version: Blender has a macOS-specific version available. To download the installer, click on the macOS link.

STEP 2: Open the Installer

- Find the Downloaded File: In your Downloads folder, you should be able to locate the .dmg file when the download is finished. The file should be called blender-4.2.0-macOS.dmg.
- Get the DMG file open. To open the .dmg file, double-click on it. By doing this, the disk image will mount and the Blender program icon will appear in a new window.

STEP 3: Install Blender 4.2

- Drag Blender to Applications: Move the Blender icon to the Applications folder shortcut by dragging it into the window that displays. By copying Blender to your Applications folder, you may access it just like any other installed program.
- Close the Installer Window: Once the copy is finished, you may use the Finder's "Eject" option or drag the disk image to the Trash to remove it from the installer.

STEP 4: Launch Blender 4.2

- Unlock the Blender: Locate Blender by going to your Applications folder and selecting it. Press Double-Click to open Blender.
- Ignore Security Warnings: Blender may present a warning that it was downloaded from the internet when you first run it. This is a common security feature included in macOS. To ensure that you wish to open the program, click "Open".
- Choose Keymap (Optional): Blender may ask you to select a keymap (Blender's default, industry standard, etc.) when you first open it. Make your choice and go forward.

STEP 5: Verify Installation

- Check Blender Version: You may use the top menu bar to navigate to Blender > About Blender or the splash screen that appears when the program first launches to confirm the installed version of Blender.
- Examine the User Interface: Become acquainted with Blender's settings and user interface. You may customize Blender to fit your workflow by changing its options.

Troubleshooting

- Permissions Problems: Verify that you have administrator rights on your Mac in case you run into permission problems during installing.
- Protector of the Gates Caution: Blender may not open if macOS Gatekeeper is unable to validate the developer. In such circumstances, choose "Open Anyway" for Blender under System Preferences > Security & Privacy > General.
- Performance and Graphics: To prevent graphical hiccups or performance problems, make sure your macOS and graphics drivers are up to date.

> **System Requirement For macOS**

	Recommended	Minimum
OS	macOS 14 (Sonoma)	macOS 11.2 (Big Sur)
CPU	Apple Silicon	Apple Silicon/ Intel
RAM	32 GB	8 GB
GPU		GPU with Metal 2.2

> **Installing on Linux**

Depending on the distribution you're running, there are subtle differences in how to install Blender on a Linux machine. Nonetheless, installing the program and downloading it are the standard procedures. This is a step-by-step tutorial that walks you through installing Blender 4.2 on a Linux computer, with special instructions for Fedora and Ubuntu.

STEP 1: Download Blender

- Go to the Blender website: Go to Blender's official website.
- Visit the page for downloads: To get to the download page, click the "Download" button.
- Choose the Linux Version: There is a Linux version of Blender available. To get the tarball (.tar.xz file), click the Linux link.

STEP 2: Extract the Tarball

- Find the file you downloaded: The .tar.xz file you downloaded can be found in your browser's file save location or in the Downloads folder.
- Launch the Terminal: To extract the tarball, you can use the terminal or a graphical file manager. This is how you use the terminal to accomplish it:
  - Go to the directory where the downloaded file is located:
    cd ~/Downloads
  - Extract the tarball:
    tar -xf blender-4.2.0-linux-x64.tar.xz

Blender will be extracted by running this command into a directory called blender-4.2.0-linux-x64; the precise name may differ depending on the version.

STEP 3: Lunching Blender 4.2

1. Go to Blender's Directory by clicking here. Make a directory change in Blender:
   cd blender-4.2.0-linux-x64

2. Start the Blender: Launch the Blender application:
   ./blender

You may now launch Blender and start utilizing the program.

STEP 4: Creating a Desktop Shortcut (Optional)

You may construct a desktop shortcut or launcher to make it simpler to open Blender:

1. Make a file for desktop entry: Launch a text editor and make a new file with the contents listed below:
   [Desktop Entry]
   Name=Blender
   Comment=Blender 4.2
   Exec=/path/to/blender-4.2.0-linux-x64/blender
   Icon=/path/to/blender-4.2.0-linux-x64/blender.svg
   Terminal=false
   Type=Application
   Categories=Graphics;3DGraphics;

Replace /path/to/blender-4.2.0-linux-x64/ with the actual path to your Blender directory.

2. Save the File: Save the file with a .desktop extension, for example, blender.desktop.
3. Turn on the file's execution: Declare a file executable:
   chmod +x blender.desktop
4. Transfer the File to the Applications Folder: Transfer the desktop icon to the relevant directory:
   mv blender.desktop ~/.local/share/applications/

STEP 5: Updating Blender

You may update Blender by downloading the most recent tarball, extracting it, and then doing the setup and extraction instructions again when a new version becomes available.

Troubleshooting

- Dependencies: Verify that your system has what it needs, including the appropriate versions of OpenGL and other libraries. Your package manager may often be used to install any missing dependencies.
- Permissions: You might need to use sudo to execute some tasks if you run into permission problems.
- Graphics Drivers: To prevent graphical glitches or performance problems, make sure your graphics drivers are up to date.

CHAPTER 2: User Interface

⊥ Splash Screen

Blender displays a splash screen in the middle of the window when it first launches. It offers the ability to start fresh projects or open old ones. A more thorough explanation is provided below.

Click anyplace around the splash screen (but within the Blender window) or hit Esc to exit it and begin a new project. The default screen will become visible once the splash screen vanishes. Click the Blender symbol in the Topbar and choose Splash Screen to bring up the splash screen once more.

⊥ Top Bar

Blender 4.2's Topbar is a crucial component of the user interface, offering instant access to key features and configuration options. It extends over the top of the Blender window and has a number of tools and menus to help with productive working. Below is a summary of the Topbar's primary elements and functionalities:

➢ Main Menus

🔴 File   Edit   Render   Window   Help

- **File:** You may save and export your work using this menu, as well as create new files and open old ones. It also has settings for importing and exporting different formats, accessing user preferences and add-ons, and connecting and appending data from other Blender files.
- **Edit:** You may undo and redo activities, copy and paste, and access settings using the tools available in the Edit menu. It also has possibilities to change input setups and themes, among other things.
- **Render:** You may choose how your scene will be rendered as an animation or as a picture using this menu. The render view and render settings are also accessible.
- Window: This is where you control Blender's window management, including switching between full-screen and workspace modes.
- Help: The Help menu contains connections to community forums, the Blender handbook, and other support materials. It is a useful tool for locating help.

➢ **Workspace Tabs**

The workspace menus have tabs just beneath them. You may transition between many workspaces using these tabs, each one designed for a particular purpose, such as UV editing, shading, animation, modeling, sculpting, rendering, compositing, and scripting. Workspaces can be added, changed, or removed as needed.

➢ **Tool Settings**

Options unique to the tool that is now selected are available in the Tool Settings panel, which is often located on the right side of the Topbar. With parameters and settings that may be changed for exact control over your activities, this panel adjusts itself based on the active tool. For instance, the Tool Settings allow you to easily adjust the brush's size, strength, and falloff.

➢ **Scene Information And Settings**

- Scene Selection: This feature lets you move between scenes in a single Blender project.
- View Layer: You may utilize many view layers to arrange and render different portions of your scene independently.
- Select from a variety of render engines, such as Cycles, Eevee, and others. Performance and rendering quality are impacted by this parameter.
- Access and modify camera and render settings quickly, including the current camera for rendering.

➢ **Contextual Menus and Operators**

The Topbar may show other menus and operators related to the current task, depending on the mode and context. For example, you could see brush-specific choices in Sculpt Mode and playback and keyframing options in Animation Mode.

➢ **Quick Search and Navigation**

A search bar is frequently included in the Topbar to aid in locating tools, commands, and settings fast. When it comes to accessing functions without having to go through several menus, this feature is really helpful.

➢ **Customization and Accessibility**

The Topbar and the Blender interface are both quite customizable. To suit your workflow, you may reorder pieces, conceal or expose particular menus, and change the layout. Whether you're interested in modeling, animation, or any other area of 3D development, Blender's customizable interface allows you to tailor it to your requirements.

➤ **Workspaces**

Blender 4.2 workspaces are customized settings made to maximize your productivity for particular jobs. The way that editors and panels are arranged in each workspace takes into account the many facets of the 3D development process. An overview of the default workspaces and instructions for managing and modifying them to suit your requirements can be found here.

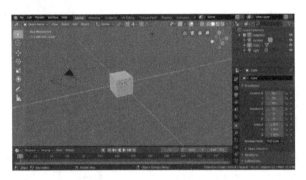

> ➤ **Default Workspace**

1. Layout
   - General-purpose workspace for basic operations, scene setup, and 3D modeling.
   - Editors: Timeline, Properties, Outliner, and 3D Viewport.
   - Use: Perfect for basic modeling, object handling, and scene setup.
2. Modeling:
   - Purpose: Focused on detailed 3D modeling tasks.
   - Editors: 3D Viewport with a tool shelf, Outliner, Properties, and a smaller Timeline.
   - Usage: Optimized for creating and editing mesh objects with modeling tools.
3. Sculpting:
   - Purpose: Dedicated to digital sculpting and high-detail modeling.
   - Editors: 3D Viewport with sculpting tools, Tool Settings, and a smaller Outliner.

- Usage: Provides access to various brushes and sculpting options for high-resolution detail work.
4. UV Editing:
   - Purpose: Specialized for UV mapping and texture editing.
   - Editors: 3D Viewport and UV/Image Editor side by side.
   - Usage: Facilitates unwrapping 3D models and editing UV maps for texturing.
5. Texture Paint:
   - Purpose: Designed for painting textures directly onto 3D models.
   - Editors: 3D Viewport, UV/Image Editor, and Tool Settings.
   - Usage: Access to painting tools and options for creating detailed textures.
6. Shading:
   - Purpose: Focused on creating and editing materials and shaders.
   - Editors: 3D Viewport, Shader Editor, and a smaller Outliner.
   - Usage: Node-based workflow for creating complex materials.
7. Animation:
   - Purpose: Optimized for creating and editing animations.
   - Editors: 3D Viewport, Timeline, Dope Sheet, and Graph Editor.
   - Usage: Keyframe animation, managing animation curves, and fine-tuning motion.
8. Rendering:

- Purpose: Focused on rendering scenes and adjusting render settings.
- Editors: 3D Viewport, Properties, and Image Editor.
- Usage: Preview renders, adjust render settings, and manage render outputs.

9. Compositing:
- Purpose: For post-processing and compositing rendered images and animations.
- Editors: Node Editor, Image Editor, and a smaller 3D Viewport.
- Usage: Node-based compositing for adding effects and combining images.

10. Scripting:
- Purpose: Dedicated to scripting and automation using Python.
- Editors: Text Editor, 3D Viewport, and Console.
- Usage: Write and test Python scripts to extend Blender's functionality.

➢ Managing and Customizing Workspaces

Creating a New Workspace:

- Add Workspace: Click the "+" button next to the existing workspaces.
- Choose Template: Select a template or start from an existing workspace.
- Customize Layout: Arrange editors and panels to fit your workflow.
- Save Workspace: Name your workspace and save it for future use.

Modifying an Existing Workspace:

- Drag and Drop Editors: Rearrange editors by dragging their headers.
- Split/Join Areas: Right-click the border between editors to split or join areas.
- Adjust Editor Types: Change the type of editor by clicking the editor's header and selecting a new type.
- Save Changes: Blender automatically saves your workspace layout, but you can also save it as part of your startup file (File > Defaults > Save Startup File).

Switching Workspaces:

- Workspace Tabs: Click on the workspace tabs at the top of the Blender window.
- Shortcut Keys: Use shortcut keys (Ctrl + Page Up/Page Down) to switch between workspaces quickly.

Deleting a Workspace:

- Right-Click Tab: Right-click on the workspace tab you want to delete.
- Delete Workspace: Select "Delete Workspace" from the context menu.

Status Bar

Blender 4.2's Status Bar may be found at the bottom of the Blender window. It helps you keep informed about the progress of your project and streamlines some processes by offering rapid access to a variety of features and useful information. Below is a comprehensive rundown of the elements and functionalities of the Status Bar:

> **Component of the Status Bar**

1. Active Tool and Tool Settings

- Description: Shows the active tool along with its main settings.
- Use: Access key settings and quickly check which tool is active without leaving the 3D Viewport or other editors.

2. Selection Info:
   - Description: Shows information about the current selection, such as the number of selected vertices, edges, faces, or objects.
   - Usage: Helpful for keeping track of what you have selected, especially in complex scenes or while editing meshes.

3. Scene Statistics:
   - Description: Provides an overview of the scene, including the total number of objects, vertices, edges, faces, and other elements.
   - Usage: Useful for monitoring the complexity of your scene and ensuring optimal performance.

4. Active Object Information:
   - Description: Displays the name and type of the currently active object.
   - Usage: Helps you quickly identify the active object and switch context if needed.

5. Playback Controls:
   - Description: Controls for playing, pausing, and navigating through the timeline.
   - Usage: Essential for animation work, allowing you to preview and scrub through your animations directly from the Status Bar.

6. Message Area:
   - Description: Displays contextual messages, warnings, and error notifications.

- Usage: Keeps you informed about important events, such as successful operations, errors, or warnings that require your attention.
7. Context-Sensitive Options:
   - Description: Provides additional options and information based on the current context and active tools.
   - Usage: Enhances workflow efficiency by offering quick access to relevant functions and settings.

⊹ Regions

In Blender, each Editor is separated into regions. Smaller organizing components, such as tabs and panels with buttons, controls, and widgets positioned inside of them, can be included into regions.

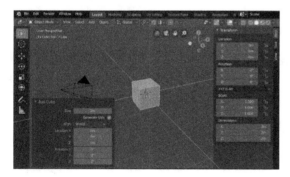

➢ Main Region

There is always at least one visible zone. It is the most noticeable area of the editor and is referred to as the Main section.

The primary region and the availability of supplementary areas vary between editors due to their distinct purposes. See the Editors chapter for further information on each editor.

➢ Header

A header is a narrow strip of horizontal text that appears at the top or bottom of a section. Every editor has a header that houses frequently used tools and menus. Depending on the type of editor, the item and mode selected, menus and buttons will alter.

➢ **Toolbar**

Interactive tools are located in the Toolbar, which is located on the left side of the editing area. T changes the Toolbar's visibility on and off.

➢ **Tool Settings**

A horizontal bar with the tool's settings now chosen that sits at the top or bottom of the editor, resembling the header. It has the same context menu functionality as the header, allowing for movement and hiding.

➢ **Adjust Last Operation**

An operator can be adjusted after it has been executed by using the Adjust Last Operation area. You can adjust the size of a cube, for instance, by using this region if it was just introduced.

➢ **Side Bar**

Panels with options for both the editor and its own objects may be found in the Sidebar, which is located on the right side of the editor area. N changes the Sidebar's visibility on and off.

➢ **Footer**

Certain editors have a bar that shows information about the active tool or operator, for example, at the top or bottom of the editor area.

➤ **Arranging**

Scrolling

Using the MMB, a section may be dragged vertically or horizontally to scroll. The Wheel may also be used to scroll a region without a zoom level by dragging it with the mouse while it is in the hover state.

Certain areas—animation timelines, for example—have scrollbars with extra control points to change the region's vertical or horizontal range. The ends of these unique scrollbars will include extra widgets, as seen in the picture below:

With this, you may adjust the range to display a greater or lesser detail in the given screen area. To change the range that is displayed, just drag one of the dots. By dragging in the editor with Ctrl + MMB, you may also rapidly change the range in both the horizontal and vertical directions.

✛ **Tabs and Panels**

➤ **Tabs**

The user interface's overlapping portions are managed with tabs. Only one Tab's content is displayed at once. A tab header, which can be vertical or horizontal, contains a list of tabs.

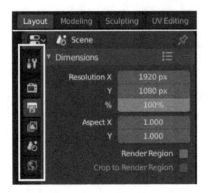

Switching or Cycling

Ctrl+Wheel may be used to flip between vertical tabs from anyplace in the tab. Additionally, you may use Shift+Ctrl+Tab and Ctrl+Tab to cycle across tabs, or you can use LMB to depress the mouse and drag it over each of the tab heading icons.

➢ Panels

A panel is the smallest structural element in the user interface. The panel's title is displayed in the panel header. It is constantly apparent. Subpanels are also included in certain panels.

• Position

A panel's location inside its area may be adjusted by clicking on and dragging on the grip widget (::::) located on the header's right side.

• Pinning

It can be useful to simultaneously examine panels from several tabs at times. For example, being able to view the attributes of a camera while other items are selected. The solution to this is to enable pinnability for panels.

Whichever tab is picked does not affect the visibility of a pinned panel. By selecting the pin icon located in the panel's header, you may pin it. Panels without a pin symbol can be pinned by holding down Shift-LMB or right-clicking on the panel header and choosing Pin.

> **Presets**
- **Selector**

A selection of the available settings. The bundled properties will be superseded by a selection.

- **Add +**

Based on the set of attributes that are now applied, new presets can be added and saved for later use. When a pop-up window appears, you may choose a name from the list and, in some situations, modify other parameters.

- **Remove –**

Removes the chosen setting.

↓ **Shortcuts**
> **Keyboard Shortcuts**

This handbook displays hotkey letters as they would look on a keyboard, such as:

- **G**is referring to the lowercase g.
- **Ctrl, Shift, Alt**
  Are specified as modifier keys.
- **Ctrl+W, Shift+Alt+A**
  Suggests that pressing these keys at the same time is recommended.
- **Numpad0-Numpad9, NumpadPlus**
  Refer to the keys that is on the separate numeric keypad.

- Some other keys are referred to by their names, such as **Esc, Tab, F1 to F12**. Of special note are the arrow keys, **Left, Right** and others.

➢ **Mouse**

Mouse buttons are referred to in this document as:

- **LMB**
  Left Mouse Button
- **RMB**
  Right Mouse Button
- **MMB**
  Middle Mouse Button
- **Wheel, WheelUp &WheelDown**
  Scrolling the wheel.

➢ **Hovering**

While the pointer is lingering (over a button).

Properties

- Ctrl + C: Copy the selected value of the button.
- Ctrl + V: Paste the selected value of the button.
- Ctrl + Alt + C: Copy the whole color of vector of the field.
- Ctrl + Alt + V: Paste the whole color of the field.
- RMB: Open the menu of the context.
- Backspace: Delete the value.
- Minus: Translate number values (multiply by -1.0).
- Ctrl + Wheel: Change the incremental value steps.

  For pop-up option menus buttons, this cycles the value.

- Return: Turn on menus or toggles the value.

- Alt: In order to make changes to all of the chosen items, hold down when altering values. (objects, bones, sequence-strips).

Number fields and toggles these shortcuts can be use.

> ## Animation

- I: Input a keyframe.
- Alt + I: Delete the keyframe.
- Shift + Alt + I: Delete all keyframes.
- Ctrl + D: Assigning a driver.
- Ctrl + Alt + D: Delete the driver.
- K: Inserting a Keying Set.
- Alt + K: Deleting the Keying Set.

> ## Python Scripting

- Ctrl + C: When you hover over any Operational Buttons, the corresponding Python command is copied to the clipboard. You may use this in the Text editor or Python Console to write scripts.
- Shift + Ctrl + C: Their data path for this property is copied by hovering over property buttons.
- Shift + Ctrl + Alt + C: Overproperty buttons replicate the data-block and property's entire data flow. Keep in mind that it is usually preferable to retrieve items by context rather than by name.

> ## Dragging

- Ctrl: Snap to discrete steps, when dragging.
- Shift: This gives control over values in the field.
- Shift + Ctrl: The item will be precisely moved by precise snap in addition to the snapping limitation.

➢ **Text Editing**

- Home: Move to the beginning of the line.
- End: Move to the ending part of the line.
- Left, Right: Take the cursor for a single move.
- Ctrl + Left, Ctrl + Right: Take the cursor for an entire word.
- Backspace, Delete: Remove characters.
- Ctrl + Backspace, Ctrl + Delete: Remove words.
- Shift: Choose while pressing down the key and moving the cursor.
- Ctrl + A: Choose all text.
- Ctrl + C: Copy the highlighted text.
- Ctrl + X: Cut the highlighted text.
- Ctrl + V – Paste text at the position of the cursor.

⊥ Buttons

Operator Buttons

When an operator button is pressed with LMB, an operator is executed, which, in essence, performs an operation. Operator buttons can be text, an icon, or an icon combined with text.

Toggle Buttons and Checkbox

Options can be activated or deactivated using these controls. To alter their status, use LMB. Checkboxes with a tick indicate that the option is active. Toggle buttons' active status is shown by a change in icon images or a change in color on the icon backdrop.

Dragging

You may drag over numerous buttons while holding down the LMB button to turn multiple settings at once on or off. This may be used to choose a radio button value, toggle buttons, and checkboxes.

⊹ Fields
➢ Search and Text Field

Text fields have a rectangular border that is rounded, and they may also have an icon or text inside of them. Text fields are used to store text strings and offer conventional text editing shortcuts for text editing.

➢ Number Field

Units and values are stored in number fields.

When the mouse pointer is above the first kind of number field, angles indicating left (<) and right (>) are displayed on the field's sides.

A second kind of number field is called a slider, which shows numbers throughout a range, such as percentage values, with a colored bar in the backdrop.

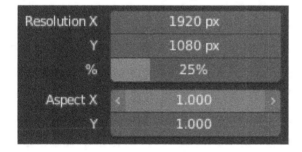

➢ Multi-value Editing

By holding down **LMB** on the first field and dragging vertically over the fields you wish to modify, you may edit several number fields at once. Lastly, you have two options: release the LMB and put in a valueor use the mouse to drag left or right to alter the value.

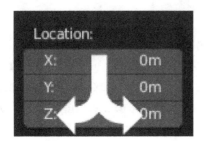

> **Value Limit**

"Soft limit" and "hard limit" value ranges limit the majority of numerical values. Only the "soft limit" value range may be changed by dragging with the mouse. Wider value ranges can be used when entering data via a keyboard, but they can never go above the "hard limit."

> **Color Field**

A color value is kept in the color field. Using LMB to click on it brings up the Color Picker.

Alpha channel color fields are split in half: the color is displayed without an alpha channel on the left, and with an alpha channel over a checkerboard pattern on the right. You may drag and drop colors to other color areas to copy them.

When you hover your cursor over a color attribute, a huge preview of the color and its RGBA, HSVA, and hexadecimal values will appear.

Decorators

Small buttons called decorators that display the property's condition are positioned to the right of other buttons. Checkboxes, menus, and number fields may all have decorators next to them to show that the feature is animated.

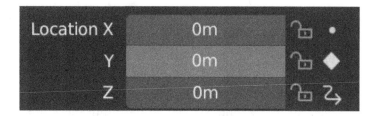

Location X	0m	🔓	•
Y	0m	🔓	◆
Z	0m	🔓	⤶

When the decoration dot icon is clicked, a Key-frame is added to that property. To eliminate the key-frame, simply click the rhombus icon once again. When a rhombus icon is solid, it means that a key-frame is present on the current frame; when it is not solid, it means that the attribute has a key-frame on a different frame. A key-frame with the currently selected value will be created on the current frame when you click the non-solid rhombus symbol.

The decorator displays the driver icon when one property is being driven by another.

Decorators streamline the process of quickly assessing a property's condition.

⊹ Color Picker

You may provide a color value using the color picker, a pop-up window. To quickly choose primary colors, hold down the Ctrl key while dragging.

- Palette
  Allows you to select the primary and secondary color elements. You can alter the shape; see to Types.
- Slider for Colors
  The third color part may be defined using the gradient-background slider. The Wheel may also be used to control it.
- Model Color

Choose the Color Model for the following numerical fields.

HSV/HSL, Hex, and RGB

⊹ Curve Widget

Using a curve with the X and Y axes representing the input and output, the Curve Widget makes it simple to transfer an assortment of value inputs to a set of output values.

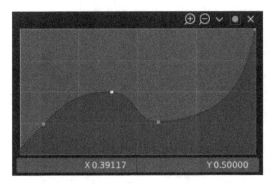

Control points

Control points are used to manipulate the Curve Widget's curve, much like they do with any other Blender curve.

In other words, the input is mapped exactly to the output (unchanged) at (0.0, 0.0) and (1.0, 1.0), where there are two control points by default.

⊹ Node

In Blender, every node has a similar foundation. This is true for all kinds of nodes. These components include of the attributes, sockets, title, and more.

Inputs

The node's inputs, which are on its bottom left, supply the information required for the node to function. When unplugged, each input socket—aside from the green shader input—has a default value that may be changed via a color, numeric, or vector interface input. A color interface input determines the second color choice in the node screenshot above.

Certain nodes are equipped with unique sockets that support several inputs. Instead of a circle, these sockets will have an ellipsis to represent their unique behavior.

Output

The node's upper right section has its outputs, which can be linked to nodes lower in the node tree via their inputs.

> **Frame Node**

By assembling similar nodes in one location, the Frame node helps organize nodes. When a node arrangement grows complicated and extensive, frames come in handy, although they are not necessary if a node group may be reused.

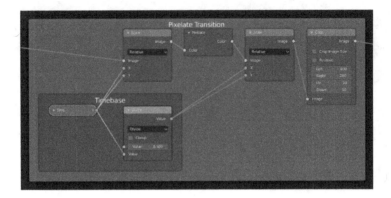

- Label Dimensions

Label font size. For instance, smaller titles for subordinate frames.

- Diminish

The frame shrinks around a node after it is inserted to eliminate unnecessary space. Resizing of the Frame now happens automatically as nodes inside it are rearranged; it is no longer necessary to pick the edge of the Frame to resize it. Disabling this option will alter this behavior.

- Text

Frame nodes can show a text data-block's contents when you need to present text that is more thorough. You will have to edit the contents using the Text Editor because this is read-only.

> **Reroute Node**

A node is a structure that is mostly utilized for organizing. In that it allows numerous output connections while supporting just one input connection, reroute functions and looks a lot like a socket on other nodes.

Holding Shift and RMB while sweeping across the link will add a Reroute node to an existing connection rapidly.

⊕ Operators

Activating an operator initiates an action; this distinguishes operators from tools, which need input. Popup menus, menu searches, or operator buttons can all be used to initiate an operator. Operators can be used to add, remove, or change an object's shading from sharp to smooth.

Operator Properties

The majority of operators have attributes that can be changed to improve the outcome. Modify the attributes in the Adjust Last Action section after running the operator (which will utilize its default settings).

Modal Operators

Between normal operators and tools, there is a notion known as modal operators. They need interactive input of some kind.

With LMB or Return, a modal operator's activity may be verified. Use Esc or RMB to cancel a modal operator.

Slider Operators

In the editor's Header, a percentage number may be interactively changed using slider operators.

Drag the slider to the left or right to change the percentage. Holding Ctrl will make this coarser (snapping in 10% increments), and holding Shift will make it more precise. You can use the letter E to toggle "overshoot" on several sliders, allowing you to move outside of the 0–100% range.

CHAPTER 3: Editors

⚓ Startup Scene

The startup scene appears in the 3D Viewport after the splash screen closes (assuming no other blend-file was loaded). The opening scene can be altered.

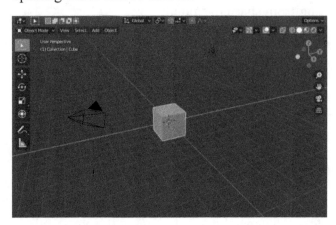

> ### Elements

- Cube

A mesh object is the gray cube in the scene's center. It is selected as shown by its orange outline. Its exact location is shown by the orange dot at the center, which is called its Origin.

- Brightness

The light source that illuminates the cube is the collection of concentric black rings.

- Snapshot

The camera, which serves as the rendering point of view, is represented by the pyramid with the large triangle perched over it.

- 3D Pointer

The location of newly inserted items is shown by the 3D pointer, which is a cross with a red and white circle. It may also be used as a pivot point for transformations.

- Grid Surface

The world's zero height is shown by the gray lines that make up the floor. The axes of the global coordinate system are represented by the red and green lines. They meet at the origin of the planet, which is also the location of the Cube's genesis. The overlays viewport popover is where you find the Grid Floor settings.

- Text Details

For more information, see Viewport Overlays. Various bits of information are displayed in the upper left corner of the viewport.

⊥ Object Mode

Modes let you alter several features of an object. You can position, rotate, and scale them in Object Mode; you can alter their geometry in Edit Mode; you can pose them in Pose Mode, and so on.

The 3D Viewport header's Mode selection can be used to alter the mode that is currently in use. The type of item determines the accessible modes. Below is a list of everything on it.

In addition to using the picker, you may also quickly access items by pressing Ctrl-Tab, which displays a pie menu around the cursor. (This shortcut will alternate between item Mode and Pose Mode if the chosen item is a Armature.)

Toggle Editing Mode on items that support it by pressing Tab.

In Blender, modes may impact several aspects:

- Every mode displays a different collection of menus and tools by altering the header and Toolbar. Thus, it also has an impact on the keyboard shortcuts that are available.
- Modes allow you to alter the viewport's appearance entirely. For instance, the object's vertex weights, which are ordinarily hidden, will be seen by shading it while using the Weight Paint mode.
- Editors might be impacted by modes. For instance, the 3D Viewport must be in Edit Mode in order to utilize the UV Editor. There are other buttons and panels in the Properties editor that are limited to particular modes of operation.

➤ **Object Mode List**

Icon	Name	Details
	Object Mode	The standard mode, appropriate for all kinds of objects. enables duplicating objects, adjusting scale, rotation, and location, among other features.
	Edit Mode	A mode for manipulating the form of an object (e.g., points/strokes for Grease Pencil, control points for curves/surfaces, vertices/edges/faces

for meshes, etc.).

	Sculpt Mode	Gives users another set of tools to change an object's form (but just for meshes).
	Vertex Paint Mode	An exclusive mode for meshes that lets you "paint" or customize the colors of its vertex sets.
	Weight Paint Mode	A mode limited to mesh that is used for vertex group weighting.
	Texture Paint Mode	A mesh-only mode that lets you use the 3D Viewport to paint a texture directly onto the object.
	Particle Edit Mode	An editable system (hair) can benefit from this mesh-only mode for particle systems.
	Pose Mode	A pose-only mode using just the armature.
	Draw Mode	A mode exclusive to the Grease Pencil that is meant for producing Grease Pencil strokes.

> **Multi-Object Editing**

Because many objects may be in Edit Mode and Pose Mode at once, working with numerous objects is considerably easier than it is in the previous description.

There are two approaches to doing this:

- To enter the mode if you haven't already, just pick every object and press enter.
- Once you're in the mode, you may use Ctrl-LMB to choose more items by clicking on the outliner's dot. The process is the same for removing things from the mode.

A few noteworthy points are:

- Only the details (shape keys, UV maps, etc.) of the current item will ever be displayed in the Properties editor; not all of the chosen objects will.
- Any element within an object becomes the active element when it is selected.
- The modifications you may make are restricted. For instance, you are unable to construct an edge that joins the vertices of many objects.

⥮ Navigating

You need to be able to adjust both the viewing direction and your point of view in order to operate in the three-dimensional realm that Blender employs. Although we will focus on the 3D Viewport editor, the majority of the other editors do comparable tasks. For instance, the Image editor allows you to zoom and pan.

➢ Navigation Gizmo

The editor's upper right corner is where you'll find the navigation device.

The view's current orientation is displayed via the Orbit gadget at the top. It will circle the screen if you drag it with LMB. Any axis label may be clicked to align the view with that axis. The other side of the same axis is selected by clicking on it once more.

> ➤ **Walk or Fly Navigation**

Occasionally, the built-in navigation controls might be restrictive, particularly in expansive settings like architectural models. Instead of circling around a central perspective in certain situations, it could be better to employ first-person controls, where you can gaze around while "standing" in one spot.

Flying and Walking are two such other navigation techniques that Blender provides. Either approach may be started from the View ‣ Navigation menu. You may also use Shift + Accent Grave to start your favorite (set in the Preferences).

Typical Fly/Walk use cases are as follows:

- Getting Around

  This can be an efficient technique to move about a big scene.

- Setting up a camera

 Activated from a Numpad0 camera view, the camera moves with you.

- capturing the motion of the camera

By going into camera view, turning on Auto Keying in the Timeline, playing back animations, and then turning on

Fly/Walk navigation, you may capture the route you walk. The route will be captured as keyframes from the camera, which may be utilized for rendering later.

Fly/Walk navigation cannot be managed while animation playback is in progress, therefore in order to halt playback once you've finished recording, you must first use LMB to quit the navigation.

> **Orthographic or Perspective**

This operator modifies the viewport camera's projection. Two distinct projection formats are supported by every 3D Viewport.

Perspective vision, in which far-off things look smaller, is accustomed to our eyes. Because objects with orthographic projection maintain their same size at all distances, it may first look a little strange. It feels as though you are looking at the sight from a very far distance. However, because orthographic seeing offers a more "technical" perspective on the image, it may be highly helpful in modeling and judging proportions.

> **Local View**

All of the scene's 3D objects are visible in global view. The selected item or objects are isolated in local view, making them the only ones visible in the viewer. This helps to speed up viewport performance in scenes with a lot of items or to work on things that are hidden by other objects. Since local view is contextual, it may be adjusted for each 3D Viewport.

By choosing the choice from the View menu or by using the Numpad-Slash shortcut, you may switch between the Global and Local Views.

3D Cursor

A point in space with both a position and a rotation is called a 3D cursor. It serves several different functions. It may be used, for instance, to manually place and orient the transform device (see Pivot Point and Transform Orientation) and define the locations of newly added items. A few tools additionally make use of the Cursor, such Bend.

> **Placement**

The 3D Cursor may be positioned in many ways.

The most versatile tool is the Cursor tool. To position the 3D Cursor, just choose it from the Toolbar and use LMB to click on a point in the scene. You may select the orientation of the tool in the tool settings. By default, it aligns with the view orientation, but you can alternatively align it with the transform orientation or the surface normal of a piece of geometry.

As an alternative, you may choose any tool and hit Shift + RMB. The 3D Cursor in this instance will always be oriented in line with the view.

You should employ two orthogonal, perpendicular 3D viewports for accuracy, which can be any combination of side Numpad3, front Numpad1, and top Numpad7. In this manner, you may decide on the depth in one view and manage the location along two axes in another.

The depth for the geometry beneath the cursor is utilized by default. The Pointer Surface Project toggle in the Settings may be used to deactivate this.

↓ **Display**

> **Object Type Visibility**

You may adjust which item kinds are visible and selectable using this popover. For instance, you only need to click once to turn off all of the lights in the scene.

This just affects the 3D Viewport that is open at the moment. Certain object types that are designated as unselect able remain selectable in other viewports, such as the Outliner.

> ➢ **Object Gizmos**

In the 3D Viewport, Object Gizmos provide mouse-controlled translation, rotation, and scaling. Even though they are referred to as "object" gizmos in the popover, mesh vertices and other transformable components are also covered by them.

Every surgery has its own gadget. You can use each gadget alone or in conjunction with the others.

Three color-coded axes are included on every gadget: X (red), Y (green), and Z (blue). LMB allows you to translate along an axis by dragging it. Additionally, the Move and Scale devices have tiny colored squares that allow for simultaneous transformation along two axes.

There are several modifier keys available:

- Toggle snapping and enable coarse-acceleration rotation and scaling by holding down the Ctrl key at any moment.
- To do the reverse of what is described above, hold Shift after hitting LMB. This will "slow down" the transformation in relation to mouse movement, enabling more precise changes.
- To execute the transformation in the plane perpendicular to the clicked axis, hold Shift before hitting LMB. Refer to Aircraft Locking.

The following options are available for object gizmos in the Gizmos popover:

- Orientation

The device's orientation to use. Using the viewport's transform orientation is what is meant by default. The other choices take precedence.

- Move
  To control the location, show the device. The viewing plane may be moved freely by dragging the little white circle.

- Rotate
  To regulate the rotation, show the device. Rotating around the viewing direction is possible by dragging the huge white circle. Trackball rotation is accomplished by dragging the translucent white disc (seen only when hovering above the device) inside that circle.

- Measurement
  Display the device to operate the scale. Using all three axes, drag the region between the tiny and big white circles scales.

➢ **Viewport Shading**

Blender has many shading modes to assist with various tasks. For instance, rendered shading works well for lighting setup, whereas solid shading works better for modeling.

The drop-down button opens a popover with more settings explained below, and the radio buttons allow you to adjust the shading mode.

To change the shading mode, press Z to bring up a pie menu. To transition between the current shading mode and Wireframe, press Shift-Z.

⬥ **Viewport Rendering**

Quick preview renderings can be produced using viewport rendering, as opposed to conventional renders, which originate from the active camera.

Viewport Render may be used to render animations as well as pictures.

A comparison of the final render produced using the Cycles Renderer and the Viewport render can be seen below.

➢ Settings

Viewport Render mostly makes use of the viewport's current parameters. The render engine attributes, which are where the view is rendered, contain some parameters.

Workbench render parameters are used in Solid mode; EEVEE render settings are used in Material Preview mode.

Furthermore, the following output options are also used:

- Resolution
- Aspect
- Path of output
- Format for files

➢ Rendering

Rendering from the active view is what happens when you activate Viewport Render. This implies that a virtual camera is utilized to match the current viewpoint if you are not in an active camera view. Use Numpad0 to access the active camera view in order to obtain an image from the camera's point of view.

Use Esc to stop it, just like you would with any other render.

- Rendering a Motionless Picture

A still image may be rendered using 3D Viewport. View ›
Viewport Render a picture.

- Rendering an Animation

3D Viewport may be used to render an animation. Viewport Render Animation is available.

⊹ Image Editing

➢ Overlay

The overlays that appear over photographs may be customized using the Overlays pop-over. There is a button in the header to disable the Image Editor's overlays altogether. Additionally, this option toggles whether UDIM tile information is shown.

Depending on the Image Editor mode, different choices are displayed in the pop-over. There are the following possible overlay categories:

- Geometry

UVs of Display Texture Paint

Show the UVs of the current item. For the UVs to be visible, the current object must be in either Texture Paint Mode or Edit Mode and the Image Editor must be in Paint mode.

- Picture

Display Metadata

Shows the selected render result's information. To modify the metadata to be included, view the Metadata panel on the Output tab.

CHAPTER 4: UV Editors

UV maps, which specify how a 2D picture should be mapped onto a 3D object, are edited using the UV Editor.

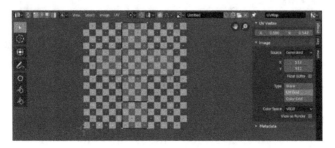

When procedural textures are not homogeneous or it is difficult to create the desired look, image textures are usually required. For instance, a car's body would not be covered with haphazard scratches; rather, they would only appear in strategic locations.

Many projections (Box, Sphere, etc.) that Blender offers may be used to automatically apply a 2D picture to a 3D object, however they are usually limited to basic meshes. For more intricate ones, a UV map must be made instead. This is a flat region where the 2D picture's faces of the 3D objects are arranged, indicating which portion of the image should be used as its texture. You now have total control over the mapping procedure.

The map's axes—V for vertical and U for horizontal—are denoted by the term "UV." These characters were used to prevent misunderstanding with the letters "X" and "Y," which instead denote 3D axes.

UV mapping is best explained by tearing apart a cardboard box. It could be stretched out flat on a tabletop if you took a pair of scissors and sliced along its edges. We may argue that U is the left-right orientation and V is the up-down direction when you gaze down at the table.

The next step may be to lay the unfolded box on top of a poster, trim the poster to fit the box's dimensions, adhere the poster to the box using glue, and then put the box back together. Now you have a 2D picture that is textured on a 3D box.

The arrangement of the box on the poster and its cutting pattern are shown in a UV map. You have total control over how this is done; if you'd want, you can even cut each side of the box separately and arrange, scale, rotate, and even skew it on the poster separately from the other sides.

Example

A dome in three dimensions flattens into a disk in ultraviolet space in the image above. Next, each 3D face is textured using the UV map portion of the picture that it covers.

The picture also shows distortion, a typical issue with UV mapping. Observe how the checkered squares in the 2D texture have the same size throughout, but when applied to the 3D dome, they take on varied sizes—they are smaller at the top than at the base. This is because, as a result of the flattening process, the faces in the UV map have different relative sizes than in 3D space.

Usually, you'll want to reduce this distortion by hand-guiding and fine-tuning the flattening—you might use seams, for instance. It isn't always feasible to get rid of it entirely, though.

✚ 2D Cursor

The UV Editor features a Cursor that you may jump to (View ‣ Center View to Cursor), just like the 3D Viewport. It can also be used as a snapping target and a pivot point.

Press Shift + RMB with any tool chosen, or LMB with the Cursor tool selected, to adjust the Cursor's location. Additionally, you have the option to modify the "Location X/Y" fields in the Sidebar's View tab using either pixel values or relative coordinates (0 to 1). The origin (0, 0) is located in the lower left corner of the picture in both scenarios.

To bring the cursor to the middle, press Shift + C.

✚ Overlays

There's a button in the header to disable the UV Editor's overlays altogether. Additionally, this option toggles whether UDIM tile information is shown.

The drop-down menu displays a pop-up with more settings in-depth. There are the following categories available:

- Grid
  Display the grid.
- Above Image
  Instead of behind the image, display the grid on top of it.
- Source of Grid Shape
  How counts are calculated for rows and columns.

✛ Selecting

The UV Editor features a Select menu and buttons for selecting modes in the header, just like the 3D Viewport.

➢ Sync Selection

The UV Editor only displays the faces that are chosen in the 3D Viewport when it is turned off, which is the default. An item is not always selected in both editors when it is selected in one. You can choose each UV vertex or edge separately if a single 3D vertex or edge corresponds to several of those.

The UV Editor always displays every face when it is switched on. When an item is selected in one editor, it is likewise selected in the other. You can only choose all of the UV vertices and edges that correspond to a single 3D vertex or edge; you cannot select individual vertices or edges.

➢ Mode of Selection

Vertex: 1 Pick out the vertices.

Edge: Two chosen edges.

Face: Three chosen faces.

Island: 4 Choose adjacent face groupings. Available only when Sync Selection is turned off.

If Sync Selection is enabled, you may expand/contract the selection by pressing Ctrl, or you can hold Shift while selecting a selection mode to activate multiple ones at once.

➢ Sticky Selection mode

Options to choose extra UV vertices automatically. Available only when Sync Selection is turned off.

- Disable

It is possible to choose each UV vertex separately from the others.

- Shared Location

UV vertices with the same UV coordinates and matching mesh vertex will be automatically selected. This is the default and creates the appearance that numerous faces in a UV map can share a vertex, whereas in fact they each have an overlap of distinct vertices.

- Mutual Vertex

Choose UV vertices that are automatically assigned to the same mesh vertex, regardless of the differences in their UV coordinates. When you activate Sync Selection, the behavior remains the same.

⊹ Snapping

UV elements may be easily aligned to other components by snapping. Toggle it on and off using the magnet icon in the UV Editor's header or, for a shorter duration, hold down the Ctrl key.

This page describes the Snap header button; see UV Editing for the Snap menu.

➢ Snap Target

- Increase

Snaps in place at grid points.

This option allows you to snap to an artificial grid with the same resolution as the editor's grid, starting at the selection's initial place. Stated differently, it allows you to shift the selection in "increments" of the size of the grid cell.

- Grid

Snaps in place at grid points.

- Vertex

Focuses on the vertex nearest to the mouse pointer.

CHAPTER 5: Objects and Scenes

Using scenes will help you arrange your work. There can be several scenes in a mix file, and these scenes can exchange objects and materials among themselves.

If you are unfamiliar with the fundamentals of Blender's Library and Data System, it is a good idea to study the instructional page before attempting to manage scenes or add or connect libraries.

⊥ Scene
- Camera

Utilized to choose the camera that is the active camera. Ctrl-Numpad0 may also be used to set the active camera in the 3D Viewport.

- Background Scene

Enables you to utilize a scene as a backdrop; this is usually helpful when you want to concentrate on animating the foreground without having background objects interfere with your work.

You may alter any of the items of this scene by selecting it from the Scene data-block menu, even though it can have its own animation and physics simulations.

Because they are recursively incorporated, Background Scenes can have Background Scenes of their own. Thus, you may always contribute to already-existing scenes by utilizing them as the backdrop for a freshly constructed scene that contains your improvements.

⊥ Objects
One or more items combine to form a scene's geometry. These items may be anything from simple 2D and 3D forms to fill your environment with models, armatures to animate those models,

lights to illuminate it, and cameras to capture photos or record a video of it all.

The two components of every Blender object type—such as a mesh, light, curve, camera, etc.—are the object and the object data, which is commonly shortened to "ObData":

> **Object Types**
- Mesh

Mesh objects may be extensively manipulated using Blender's mesh editing tools. They are made up of vertices, edges, and polygonal faces. See Primitives in Mesh.

- Bend

Mathematically defined objects whose length and curvature may be changed by manipulating them with control handles or control points rather than vertices. View Primitives Curves.

- Surface

Control points are used to alter patches that are specified mathematically. These work well for organic landscapes and basic rounded shapes. Refer to Primitives Surfaces.

- Metaball

Objects made of a mathematical function that defines the 3D volume in which it exists but has neither vertices nor control points. When two or more metaballs are brought together, they merge by gently rounding out the connection, giving the impression of being a single, cohesive item. This is the liquid-like aspect of meta things. Refer to Meta Primitives.

- Write something

Construct a two-dimensional text representation.

- Amount

Container for OpenVDB files created using Blender's Fluid Simulator or by other programs.

- Pencil Grease

Things made using brushstroke.

➤ Object Origin

There is an origin for every item. The object's position in three dimensions is determined by the location of this point. The origin point is shown by a little circle that emerges when an object is chosen. When translating, rotating, or scaling an item, the origin point's location is crucial. For more, see Pivot Points.

The origin's hue varies according on the object's selection state.

- In yellow: The object is in motion.
- Orange: The selected object is not active.
- White: The object is not chosen or connected.
- Turquoise: The object is connected.
- Pale turquoise: Though not active, the object is connected and chosen.

➤ Set Origin

It is possible to move the geometry and object origin in relation to one another and the 3D pointer.

Sort

- From Geometry to Origin

Shifts the model to the origin, causing the object's origin to coincide with its center of mass.

- From Origin to Geometry

Shifts the origin to the object's center.

- From source to 3D Cursor

Shifts the model's origin to the 3D cursor's location.

- From Origin to Center of Mass

Shifts the origin to the model's estimated center of mass (presuming a uniform mesh density).

> **Selection and the Active Object**

Which aspects will be the focus of our activities depends on selection. Selections are made for the visible things in the current scenario. Blender uses sophisticated selection techniques. In Edit Mode as well as Object Mode.

Blender differentiates between two distinct selection states:

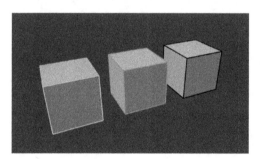

The final (de)selected item in Object Mode is referred to as the "Active Object" and is outlined in yellow (the other items are orange). At any given moment, there can only be one active item.

The active object is used as a reference by several Blender functions (such as linking operations). Use Shift-LMB to reselect an item if you already have one selected and need to make it the active one.

Just picked are all other selected items. Any number of items can be chosen. Holding Alt while confirming will allow you to modify a property or carry out an action on all chosen objects (bones and sequencer strips).

⊹ Collections

A scene may have a large number of objects: Set pieces, lighting, backgrounds, and furniture make up a standard stage scenario. Blender facilitates organization by enabling you to combine similar items into groups. Unlike parenting, objects can be grouped together without forming any type of transformation link. You may use collections to simply arrange your scene logically or to make it easier to link or attach files or scenes in one step.

➢ Collection Tabs

Convenient property access for the active collection is provided by the collection properties tab.

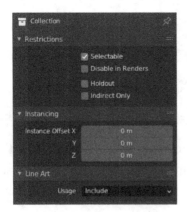

➢ Restriction

- Choose-able

Turns on and off the option to pick items from the 3D Viewport. When you have placed something in the scene and don't want to unintentionally pick it while working on something else, this is helpful.

- Turn off in Renders

Enables or disables the collection's render visibility.

- Withhold

In the active view layer, objects contained in this collection will produce a holdout or mask.

- Only Indirect

Only the shadows and reflections cast by the objects in this collection will directly affect the final image.

➤ **Instancy**

Offset of instance X, Y, Z

Applies the instanced collections' spatial offset from the origin of the original object.

➤ **Exporters**

Every collection has the option to export to multiple different file formats. These exporters are accessible worldwide, refer to Importing & Exporting Files. Nevertheless, this panel simplifies the process of repeatedly exporting the same asset or assets. For instance, it can be used to create glTFassets for a game and refine their appearance, or to create USD assets using Blender in a studio pipeline. The following file formats are supported; refer to each for the documentation of export parameters:

- Alembic
- Universal Scene Description
- Wavefront OBJ

- Stanford PLY
- FBX
- glTF 2.0

> **Line Art**

Usage

The process of loading the collection into line art. If desired, child objects inside the collection have the ability to override this option in Object Properties.

- **Add:** Produce the feature lines for this set.
- **Only Occlusion:** Only already-existing feature lines will be obscured by collection objects; their geometry will remain undetectable.
- **Exclude:** Nothing from this collection will be used to create line art.
- **Only at the Intersection:** Items in the collection don't show their own geometry; instead, they just create junction lines in the scene.
- **Absence of Intersection:** Don't create intersecting lines; just include this collection.
- **Force-Intersection:** Even when there are things preventing intersection, generate intersection lines.

Mask Collection

For the faces in this collection, use a custom intersection mask. The Line Art modifier has the ability to filter lines using intersection masks. For further information, see Collection Masks.

Mask

This mask value will be present at intersections created by this collection.

Intersection priority

Gives this collection an intersection priority value. The item with the greater intersection priority value will contain the intersection line.

⊹ View Layers

View layers have visibility settings that are intended to assist in arranging the content that you wish to see or work on.

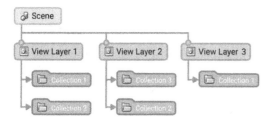

You may adjust the visibility, selectability, and other properties of view layers that are references to collections. Any collection may be enabled on a view layer, and different or the same collections can be used by several view layers.

Outliner

In the Outliner, you may modify the view layer collections.

Among other things, you may enable and disable collections as well as temporarily and worldwide conceal them.

CHAPTER 6: Modelling

Three essential elements are required to create a 3D scene: models, materials, and lighting. The first of these, modeling, is discussed in this section. To put it simply, modeling is the art and science of designing a surface that either conveys your abstract vision of items or imitates the shape of an actual object.

Modes

There are many modeling modes that you may use, depending on the kind of item you are trying to represent. Since modes are not modeling-specific, they are discussed in other sections of the handbook.

When modeling, switching between modes is typical. While certain tools might only be available in one mode, others might only be available in many modes.

Modes Editing

The primary mode used for modeling is called Edit Mode. To alter the following kinds of items, utilize alter Mode:

- Meshes
- Bends
- Surfaces
- Metaballs
- Textual elements
- Lattice

Only the items' mesh may be altered when altering them. You can utilize Multi-Object Editing, exit Edit Mode, and pick another object to alter it, among other options.

⊥ Mesh

Generally, mesh primitive shapes (such as circles, cubes, and cylinders) are used to start mesh modeling. You might then start altering to make a more intricate, bigger form.

➤ Structure

Everything in a mesh is constructed from three fundamental components: faces, edges, and vertices.

Vertices

The simplest component of a mesh is a single point or location in three dimensions, known as a vertex (plural of vertices). Small dots are used to indicate vertices in the 3D Viewport while it is in edit mode. An array of coordinates is used to store an object's vertices.

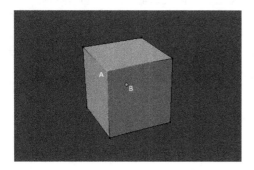

Edge

An edge is always a straight line that joins two vertices. When you see a mesh in wireframe mode, the edges are the "wires" that are visible. Usually, they are not apparent in the output picture. Faces are constructed out of them.

Faces

Faces are utilized to construct the object's real surface. When the mesh is rendered, these are what you see. In the displayed picture, this region will be translucent or nonexistent if it is devoid of faces.

A face is the region with edges on all sides that is between three (triangles), four (quadrangles), or more (n-gons) vertices. Tris, quads, and n-gons are common abbreviations for the faces.

Triangles are simple to compute since they are always flat. Quadrangles, on the other hand, "deform well," making them the favored shape for subdivision modeling and animation.

Shading

Surface Normals have a significant impact on how light interacts with three-dimensional objects, which in turn affects how those things are shaded. Normals can have flat or smooth shading.

The faces in a mesh are produced and shown consistently when flat shading is used. For things like cubes and pyramids, which have flat surfaces, this is often preferred.

Smooth shading gives a mesh a more realistic look by allowing for smooth transitions between neighboring polygons, which are done by interpolating the normals across the vertices of a polygonal mesh.

Face normal have flat shading by default, but you may change this for each face or the entire object.

> **Topology**

Loop

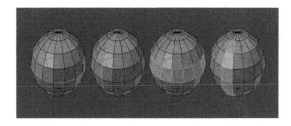

As seen in Fig., edge and face loops are collections of faces or edges that create continuous "loops." Facial and edge loops.

The loops in the preceding figure that don't terminate in a pole are cyclic (1 and 3). They split the model into two halves, beginning and ending at the same vertex. In order to deal with discrete, continuous sections of a mesh quickly and effectively, loops are a necessary component of organic character animation.

Edge Loop

The edge loops in Fig. Edge and face loops are loops (1 and 2). They join vertices so that, with the exception of the start and end vertices in the case of poles, every vertex on the loop has precisely two neighbors who are not on the loop and are positioned on both sides of the loop.

Edge loops are a crucial idea, particularly in character animation and organic (subsurface) modeling. When utilized appropriately, they let you create models with a limited number of vertices that deform well in animation and seem very natural when used as subdivision surfaces.

Consider Fig. Face loops and edges. For instance, in biological modeling, the edge loops adhere to the skin's and the underlying muscles' natural shapes and lines of deformation. In places where the figure moves more than others, like the shoulders and knees, the loops are denser.

> **Primitives**

A mesh is a typical object type found in 3D scenes. Many "primitive" mesh shapes are included with Blender so you may get started with modeling right away. Primitives can also be added using the 3D cursor in Edit Mode.

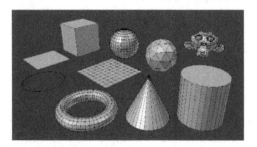

Common Options

The Adjust Last Operation panel displays when the item is created and allows you to choose these choices. Among the options found in many primitives are:

Produce UVs

Creates a new geometry's default UV unwrapping. The initial UV layer (which may be added as needed) will define this.

Size and Radius, Orient to View, Place, and Rotate

Plane

One quad face, consisting of four vertices, four edges, and one face, is the standard plane. It is similar to a sheet of paper that is resting on a table; because it is flat and lacks thickness, it cannot be considered a three-dimensional entity. Planes may be used to construct mirrors, tabletops, and floors, among other objects.

Cube

A typical cube is a three-dimensional shape with eight vertices, twelve edges, and six faces. Dice, boxes, and crates are among the items that may be made out of cubes.

UV Sphere

Quad faces plus a triangular fan at the top and bottom make up a typical UV sphere. Texturing can be done using it.

Icosphere

A polyhedral sphere composed of triangles is called an icosphere. Icospheres are typically employed to create a vertices arrangement that is more isotropical—that is, uniform in all directions—than a UV sphere.

➢ Mirrors

Mirror gives you the ability to symmetrically alter vertices along the selected axis. An element (vertex, edge, or face) will be converted in accordance with its identical axis-mirrored counterpart (in local space) if one exists, through symmetry along the selected axis.

Topology Mirror

The mirrored vertices must be precisely positioned while working on a mirrored Mesh Geometry using any of the three Mirror Axis choices. The Mirror Axis will not treat vertices as mirrored if they are not precisely positioned in their mirror positions.

Order of magnitude Mirror attempts to solve this issue by identifying mirrored vertices by examining their relationships to other vertices in the Mesh Geometry in addition to their locations. To decide which vertices will be viewed as mirrors, it considers the topology as a whole. This has the consequence of allowing non-symmetrical mirrored vertices to still be considered mirrored.

Auto Merge

When activated, vertices are automatically merged as soon as they get closer than the Threshold value. Only interactive operations are impacted by this option (tweaks done in the Adjust Last Operation window are also considered interactive). The merging will take place between the relocated vertex and one of the vertices that are present at the precise location where the vertex is moved.

> **Extrude Region**

Vertices are duplicated using extrusion tools, but the resulting geometry remains linked to the original vertices. Vertices become edges, and edges eventually become faces.

This is a crucial tool for designing novel geometries. It makes it simple to design objects like tree branches and to make parallelepipeds out of rectangles and cylinders out of circles.

It is possible to interactively set the axis that edges and vertices are extruded along. By default, faces are extruded along their mean normal. By designating an axis, the extrusion can be restricted to a single axis (see Axis Locking).

The way the new geometry is linked within the extrude tools varies.

Details

The following discussion delves into the very complex ideas that underlie Extrude, despite the technique being quite intuitive:

- Initially, the algorithm ascertains which of the chosen edges will be transformed into a face, or the outside edge loop of the extrude. Edges that belong to two or more chosen faces are regarded by the algorithm as internal by default (see below), meaning they are not included in the loop.

- Next, faces are created from the edges in the edge loop.
- All of the chosen faces are replicated and connected to the newly produced faces if the edges in the edge loop correspond to just one face in the whole mesh. At this level, rectangles, for instance, will produce parallelepipeds.
- In other scenarios, the chosen faces are not repeated, but rather connected to the recently generated faces. As a result, undesirable faces are kept from being kept "inside" the final mesh. This distinction is crucial because it guarantees that, whenever Extrude is used, consistently coherent, closed volumes are constructed.
- Extrusion only produces a duplication when it comes to fully closed volumes (such as a cube with all six faces), as the volume is replicated independently of the original.
- A "open" edge loop is formed by edges that are not part of the selected faces. These edges are duplicated, and a new face is formed by joining the new edge with the previous one.
- A new edge is formed between two single selected vertices that do not belong to any selected edges by duplicating them.

✛ Curves

Certain Blender object types are Surfaces and Curves. Instead of being stated as linear interpolation between a set of points, they are expressed as mathematical functions (interpolation).

Blender provides NURBS and Bézier curves. The "control polygon" is formed by a collection of "control points" (also known as "control vertices") that create both NURBS curves and surfaces and Bézier curves.

Although both Bézier and NURBS curves have names derived from their mathematical definitions, selecting one over the other frequently comes down to how each is internally calculated rather than how a modeler would see them. Because they begin and stop at the control points you specify, bezier curves are often easier to understand; nevertheless, when a curve has several twists and turns, NURBS curves are easier for computers to compute.

The primary benefit of utilizing curves over polygonal meshes during modeling is that curves require less data to describe and can thus provide outcomes with lower memory and storage requirements. This procedural handling of surfaces, meanwhile, may result in higher render time needs.

Curves are the sole tool available for certain modeling procedures, such extruding a profile along a route. However, curve modeling makes vertex-level control more challenging. If precise control is required, mesh editing could be a preferable modeling alternative.

The most popular curves for creating letters and logos are bezier curves.

➢ **Tools**

Type

The kind of curve to draw using.

- Poly:

Straight line segments in a Bézier curve (auto handles).

- Bézier: Tolerance

Higher numbers provide more smoothed results, while lower values produce a result that is more similar to the drawing stroke.

Technique

- Redesign:

Refit the curve incrementally to get the best results.

- Divided:

Creates a better drawing performance by splitting the curve till the tolerance is reached.

Detect Corners

Uses a given angle as a basis for corner detection while drawing; any angle greater than the given value is regarded as a corner. When a corner is identified, the curve employs non-aligned handles, which produces a corner that is more precise.

> **Transform Panels**

The panel is blank when nothing is chosen. The median values are changed and "Median" is appended before the labels when several vertices are chosen.

Control point, Vertex

The coordinates of the chosen point or handle (vertex) are displayed by the initial controls (X, Y, Z). When dealing with a NURBS curve, the weight of the chosen control point, or the median weight, is defined by the fourth component that is accessible (W).

Space

You may select whether those coordinates are relative to the global origin (global) or the object origin (local) using the Space radio buttons.

Local Global

Weight

Regulates the "goal weight" of a subset of control points. This is utilized in the case of Soft Body physics curves, which force the curve to "stick" to its initial locations in relation to the weight.

Radius

Regulates the bevel or extrusion width along the "spinal" curve. From one point to another, the radius will be interpolated (you can check it using the normals).

Tilt

Governs how each control point's normals, which are represented as arrows, twist; hence, it only matters for 3D curves! From one point to the next, the tilt will be interpolated (you can check it using the normals).

⊹ Surface

Surfaces are the 3D extension of curves, which are 2D objects. But take note that Blender only allows you to work with NURBS surfaces—no Bézier (though you may use the Bézier knot type; see below) or polygonal surfaces—you can use meshes for these instead. Curves and surfaces are not the same thing, even though they belong to the same object type (as do texts). For instance, you cannot have both curves and surfaces in the same object.

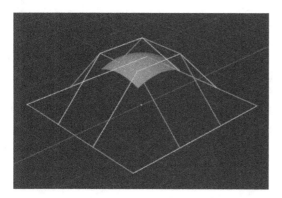

Surfaces contain two interpolation axes, U (just like curves) and V, because they are 2D. It is crucial to realize that for each one of these two dimension (the U and V fields for all these settings, naturally), you have separate control over the interpolation rules (knot, order, and resolution).

"But the surface seems to be 3D, why is it only 2D?" one may wonder. An item must have "Volume" in order to be considered three-dimensional; a surface lacks volume even when it is closed since it is endlessly thin. The surface might have a thickness (its third dimension) if it had a volume. Because of this, it can only be considered a 2D object with a maximum of two interpolation dimensions, axes, or coordinates (if you are familiar with non-Euclidean geometry, surfaces are essentially non-Euclidean 2D planes). For a more "real-world" example, try rolling a sheet of paper into a cylinder. The sheet will stay a (almost) 2D object even when it turns into a "volume"!

Visualization

NURBS surfaces in Edit Mode, there is almost no difference from NURBS curves other than the fact that the U direction is represented by yellow grid lines and the V direction is realized by pink grid lines.

Similar to curves, control points can be hidden or made visible.

Conversion

There is no "internal" conversion in this case because there are simply NURBS surfaces.

There is, however, a surface to mesh "external" conversion that is limited to using in Object Mode. It converts a surface object into a mesh object by creating faces, edges, and vertices using the surface resolutions in both directions.

> **Rows and Grid, Control Points**

The control points for NURBS curves and surfaces are the same. Their design is extremely restrictive, though. The idea of a "segment" vanishes and is replaced by "rows" and the "grid" as a whole.

A row, which is much like edge loops for meshes, is a collection of control points that create a single "line" in a single interpolation direction. In a NURBS surface, you therefore have "U rows" and "V rows." The important thing to remember is that every row of a certain kind (U or V) has the same quantity of control points. There is precisely one U row and one V row for every control point.

All of this creates a "grid," or "cage," whose form determines how the NURBS surface is shaped. Like a lattice, sort of It is crucial to understand that adding an individual control point to a NURBS surface is not possible. Instead, you must add a full U or V row at once, with precisely the same number of control points as the other rows (in reality, you will likely add them using the Extrude tool or maybe the Duplicate one). This also implies that you can only "merge" disparate surface pieces if at least one of their rows matches.

Weight

NURBS Surface control points have a weight feature, much like NURBS Splines. The control point's impact on the surface is determined by its weight characteristic. The Goal Weight, which is solely utilized for soft body simulations, should not be mistaken with this weight. In the Transform panel's W number field, the NURBS control point weight can be changed.

One control point with a weight of five is shown in Fig. The Weight of one control point, designated as "C," has been set to 5.0, while the default value for all other control points is 1.0. It is evident that the surface being drawn towards that control point.

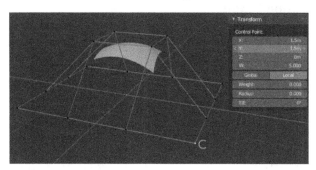

Preset Weights

Pure forms that may be created with NURBS are spheres, cylinders, and circles (a Bézier circle is not a pure circle). You have to adjust the control point weights to specified values in order to generate pure circles, spheres, or cylinders. Before doing this, you should learn more about NURBS because it is not obvious.

The idea behind creating a sphere out of 2D surfaces is the same as that of a 2D circle. It is evident that four distinct weights (1.0, 0.707 = sqrt(0.5), 0.354 = sqrt(2)/4, and 0.25) are required to create a sphere.

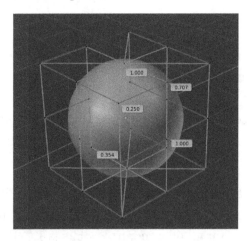

> **Shapes**

Preview Resolution U/V

Optimal resolution for the 3D Viewport.

Produce U/V

Resolution regulates the surface's level of detail, just way NURBS curves do. The surface is smoother and more detailed the higher the Resolution. The rougher the surface, the lower the Resolution. But in this case, you have two resolution settings— one for the U and V interpolation axes.

To avoid causing lag in the viewport while maintaining high-quality renders, you can independently change the resolution for both the preview and render.

✦ Metaball

Metaball objects, sometimes abbreviated as "metaball" objects, are implicit surfaces since they exist procedurally rather than being explicitly specified by vertices or control points like meshes or surfaces do. In actuality, Blender computes mathematical formulae on the fly for meta objects.

Metas are easily recognized visually because of their "rounded" shapes and fluid, mercurial, or clay-like appearances. Moreover, two meta objects start interacting with one other as they approach one another. They "blend" or "merge" similarly to how water droplets do, particularly in zero-g. This makes them incredibly useful for simulating water streams when you don't want to run a fluid simulation. Should they thereafter separate from each other, they return to their initial configuration.

You may use the Active Element panel to switch between any of them at any moment. any of these is determined by its own underlying mathematical structure.

Meta objects are typically used as a foundation for modeling or for special effects. For instance, you may start your model's shape with a group of metas and turn it into a mesh for additional modeling or sculpting. Ray tracing can also benefit greatly from the use of meta objects.

Visualization

The computed mesh and a black "selection ring" are displayed in Object Mode.

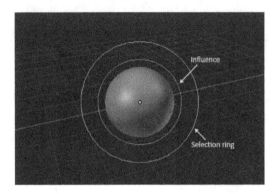

A meta is shown as a mesh (either shaded or as black wireframe, but without any vertex, of course) in Edit Mode (Fig. Meta Ball in Edit Mode). It has two colored circles: a red circle for selection (pink when selected) and a green circle for direct control of the meta's stiffness (light green when active). Keep in mind that having the green circle highlighted is the same as having the red one, save from the scale transformation.

⚜ Text

Since fonts are vector data (composed of curves), text objects are part of the same object type family as curves and surfaces.

To handle the mapping of letter codes to the geometry that represents them in the 3D Viewport, Blender employs a "Font System." This font system supports external fonts such as PostScript Type 1, OpenType, and TrueType in addition to its own built-in font. Furthermore, it may create letters out of any object that is present in the current blend-file.

With the help of text objects, you can design and show 2D or 3D text with a variety of sophisticated layout choices, such as frames and justifying. Like any closed 2D curve, letters are really just flat filled surfaces by default. However, you may extrude them and add modifiers to them, just like you would with curves (e.g. to make them follow a curve).

Blender allows for the arrangement of text in a number of rather sophisticated ways, such as by creating columns or text blocks, utilizing various alignments, and more.

➤ Text Editing

In Blender, editing text takes place primarily in two places and is very different from editing other object types. The 3D Viewport is the first place where you input text. It has a few shortcuts for applying styles, for example (see Font); nevertheless, most of the Blender shortcuts you are familiar with in Edit Mode do not apply to texts. The Properties, particularly the Font tab, come in second.

- **Cut**

Use the shortcut or the appropriate Edit menu option to cut and copy text to the buffer (Ctrl + x).

- **Copy**

Use the shortcut or the corresponding Edit menu option to copy text to the buffer (Ctrl + C).

- **Paste**

Use the shortcut or the corresponding Edit menu option to paste text from the buffer (Ctrl + v).

- **To Paste File**

Text from an external text file is inserted. This will open a File Browser so you may open a legitimate UTF-8 file. As always, take care that there aren't too many characters in the file because this can slow down interactive response (Header ▸ Text ▸ Paste File).

- **To Upper Case**

Converts the chosen text's case to uppercase (Header ▸ Text ▸ Upper Case).

- **To Lower Case**

Converts the chosen text's case to lowercase (Header ▸ Text ▸ Lower Case).

- **Insert Unicode**

Enables the input of any Unicode character by its hexadecimal codepoint value in a dialog box (Header ▸Text ▸ Insert Unicode).

- **Special Characters**

This character map is restricted to inserting characters that aren't accessible using the keyboard. You can "compose" a lot of different special characters; see Accent Characters. You'll have to copy and paste them from an external editor or character map software if you need more (Header ▸Text ▸ Special Character).

- **Applying Bold, Underline**

You may either choose the text that already exists and then toggle the chosen style from the menu, or you can switch on the corresponding setting before inputting any letters to apply the Bold, Italics, Underline, or Small Caps attribute to that set of characters.

⊥ Volume

In Blender, OpenVDB files are represented as volume objects, which are containers. A library and file format for volumetric data storage and interchange is called OpenVDB. OpenVDB files can be produced by Blender's fluid simulation cache or by other programs like Houdini.

You can generate volume objects in Blender by dragging and dropping vdb-files into the program or by using the Add menu in the 3D Viewport. An OpenVDB file's frame sequence can be loaded for animations.

Rendering Volume

Rendering smoke simulations and volumes function in the same way. Rendering volume objects by default uses the Principled Volume shader. By default, it will make use of the density, color, and temperature grids. In the shader nodes, a different grid name has to be selected if they are not accessible.

Limitations

Sparse volumes, which may be dispersed throughout space rather than necessarily contained within a small bounding box, are well-represented by OpenVDB. These are still drawn as thick volumes in Blender, which is not the best for speed or memory use. Future versions will include improvements to this.

Points and level sets can also be stored in OpenVDB files. Level set grids are readable, but as of right now, they are not supported when shown as surfaces. OpenVDB point imports are not supported.

Empties

With no extra geometry, the "empty" is only a single coordinate point that may be used for a variety of applications as a handle. However, because it lacks a surface and volume, it cannot be displayed.

> **Primitives**

- **Plain Axes**

Originally appears as six lines, one for the +X, -X, +Y, -Y, +Z, and -Z axis directions.

- **Arrows**

Appears as labeled arrows that are originally oriented in the positive X, Y, and Z axis orientations.

- **Single Arrow**

Appears as a single arrow that points in the direction of the +Z axis at first.

- **Image**

Images can be shown in empty spaces. Using this, reference pictures such as character sheets or blueprints may be produced for modeling purposes. Regardless of the 3D display setting, the picture is presented.

You can go to the Empty Displays settings from Properties ‣ Object Data ‣ Empty panel.

CHAPTER 7: Painting and Sculpting

Painting and sculpture provide a more flexible method of brush editing. There are several ways to accomplish this, each with a distinct function.

⊥ Brush

The primary tool for working with any painting or sculpting mode is the brush. Depending on the brush settings, clicking and dragging in the 3D Viewport will apply an effect and generate a stroke.

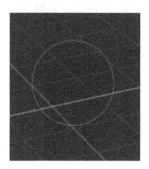

Brush Settings

The most popular keys for adjusting the brush are these ones.

- Use the F brush size.

- Brush strength setting Shift + F.
- Ctrl + F to adjust the brush's weight and rotate its texture.

You have two options for changing the value after pressing these keys: interactively or by entering in numbers. To adjust the value further with accuracy (Shift) and/or snapping (Ctrl) enabled, move the mouse right or left. Lastly, either cancel (RMB, Esc) or confirm (LMB, Return).

By holding down Ctrl, you may also reverse the brush's direction or effect.

> **Stroke**

The behavior of the painted or sculpted stroke is defined by the stroke parameters. Over the stroke, any additional brush behavior or effect is added.

Stroke Methods

Specifies how the paint is applied on the canvas using brushstrokes.

- **Dots:**

Paint every mouse movement step. This is dependent on the stroke speed rather than how far apart they are from one another. This implies that greater cumulative strength will be used with a slower stroke.

- **Drag Point:**

Just leaves one dab, which may be moved with a drag, on the canvas.

- **Area:**

Produces brush strokes in the form of a string of dots, the spacing of which is controlled by the Spacing parameter.

- **Distance:**

Restricts the amount of brush work to the distance indicated by the brush radius %.

- **Airbrush:**

Depending on the Rate option, the brush's flow will continue as long as the mouse click is held (spray).

- **From Edge to Edge:**

A two-point circle is used to identify the placement and orientation of the brush. The first click creates one point, and dragging creates the second point, which is opposite the first.

- **Line:**

To define a line in screen space, click and drag. Like space strokes, spacing is used to separate the line dabs. The line stroke is limited to 45 degree increments while using Alt.

- **Curve:**

Uses a Bézier curve to define the stroke curve (dabs are spaced based on spacing). Blender stores this Bézier curve as a "Paint Curve" data-block.

➤ **Stabilize Stroke**

Stabilize Stroke causes the stroke to trail the cursor and adds a gentle curve to its course. You may activate this by clicking the checkbox located in the header or by hitting Shift S.

- Radius

Minimum separation required before the stroke resumes from the previous position.

- Factor

Higher values of this smooth factor provide smoother strokes, but the sketching experience is still similar to tugging the stroke.

> ➢ **Visibility and Selection**

It can occasionally be difficult to paint on the required vertices in a complicated model. Let's say you want to paint a tiny portion of the Mesh and leave the rest unpainted. "Selection masking" is useful in this situation. A brush will only paint on the chosen faces or vertices when this mode is activated.

Selection masking is superior to the normal paint method in the following ways:

- Even when modifiers are engaged, the original mesh boundaries remain visible.
- Instead of going into Edit Mode, you may choose and deselect faces.

Masking Vertex Selection

You can paint exclusively on the selected vertices in this mode after selecting one or more of them. Unintentional alterations are prevented for all unselected vertices.

Face Selection Masking

Similar to vertex selection masking, face selection masking lets you pick faces and restrict the paintbrush to specific faces.

Unhide or Hide Faces

Additionally, you may use the keyboard shortcut H to conceal certain faces in Edit Mode. Next, you can paint over the faces that are still visible. Finally, you can use Alt-H to reveal the hidden faces once more.

Unhide or Hide Vertices

In vertex mask selection mode, it is not possible to selectively conceal only a subset of faces. When you switch selection modes, though, the selection gets transformed. Thus, a typical ruse is to:

- To convert the selection to faces, go to the Face selection mask mode.
- Next, hone your choices or simply conceal the faces.
- Return to the mask mode for Vertex Selection.

Vertices that belong to visible faces will always be visible thanks to hiding faces.

✚ Sculpting

While Sculpt Mode and Edit Mode both allow you to modify a model's design, they function significantly differently. Firstly, brushes are used to edit a specific region of the model rather than individual pieces like faces, edges, and vertices.

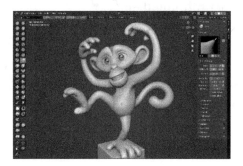

Ctrl + Tab may be used to access the pie menu or the mode menu located in the 3D Viewport header to enter Sculpt Mode. The 3D Viewport's Toolbar and Tool Settings will transform into panels exclusive to Sculpt Mode once you're in it. When the brush size is changed, the pointer will turn into a circle.

➢ The Brush

Sculpt Mode may be easily identified by the way the brush behaves and appears. The sculpting brush is shown in three dimensions, but all other brush parameters remain applicable. This indicates that by aligning the radius to match the topological Normal, the brush will follow the surface's curve.

The brush's strength may be seen by utilizing the inner ring of the brush cursor.

On order to improve tool visualization, the brush is also applied to other tools on the toolbar. The current brush radius, for instance, can be used by the Box Trim and Lasso Trim tools to adjust how deeply geometry is removed or inserted.

Common Brushes

These are the most often used brushes for sculpting, while there are many more available. More about using the Toolbar's sculpting brushes.

Clay Strips: This brush is used to build up volumes and block out large shapes before further refining them;

- Grab: This brush moves geometry across the screen for general shaping.
- Smooth: This brush smoothes and shrinks surfaces to remove noise or flatten shapes.
- Draw: This brush adds and subtracts on surfaces; it is often customized using various stroke techniques and textures for different effects.
- Scrape: This brush adds and fills surfaces for aggressive smoothing or hard surface sculpting.
- Inflate: This brush expands or contracts volumes or surfaces, particularly useful for controlling the thickness of cylindrical shapes.
- Draw Sharp: This brush is similarto Draw but has a much sharper falloff, making it useful for adding creases, cracks, and other sharp edges.

- Crease: A combination of the Pinch and Draw brushes. useful for adding further shine to already-existing creases or for producing intricate creases.
- Snake Hook: Though it works similarly to Grab, this brush will dynamically release pressure and take up geometry as it strokes. Drawing geometry out is made more easier by the fact that the dragged geometry follows the stroke's angle. Best utilized in conjunction with Dyntopo.

> **Gesture Tools**

In addition to brushes and filters, Sculpt mode includes a collection of tools that apply actions to a selected region that has been sketched. These tools have a resemblance to Blender's selection tools, such as box and lasso selection.

These tools alter the underlying mesh immediately, rather than offering a selection of parts to be altered later.

Box Gestures

The location of where LMB was pushed and released define a rectangular region that is created by dragging.

Lasso Gestures

When you drag, a freeform region is created that follows the cursor that is determined by the locations of the LMB presses and releases.

Line Gestures

A line is made by dragging. Everything on the highlighted side of the line is impacted by the ensuing action. The region that is being operated upon extends beyond the viewpoint in both directions.

Polyline Gestures

A point is placed in the viewport when you click. A new point in the polygon is formed each time LMB is pushed. The selection box closes when you hit Return or LMB on the starting point.

> ➢ **Masking, Face Set and Visibility**

Visibility Control

In Sculpt Mode, portions of the mesh can be concealed. Hideous faces are immobile, so it's simpler to focus on isolating the areas you wish to concentrate on. Viewport performance is also enhanced by hiding geometry.

With the exception of Object Mode, all modes share the feature of concealing; that is, faces hidden or seen in one mode will also be hidden in other modes.

In contrast to other painting modes where Selection Masking is used, Sculpt Mode mainly makes use of Masks and Face Sets to regulate mesh visibility and which faces may be altered at the moment. The Clipping Region is an exception, as it may be utilized in any mode.

The most often used keyboard shortcuts are Shift-H to isolate the face set under the cursor (or display everything) and H to conceal the face set under the pointer.

Using the Alt + W pie menu, you can also flip visibility and reveal everything.

The Hide Gesture Tools can also be used to change visibility.

Masks

The mesh's vertices that are affected by painting and sculpting are managed by a mask. For instance, the Mask by Color tool and Mask Gesture Tools may be used to construct and modify the mask.

The sculptmask Attributes are used internally to store masks.

Invert and Clear

The mental model used for creating masks differs somewhat from that used for selecting in other modes. For instance, smoothing is accomplished by using Shift + LMB rather than augmenting a mask.

Conceptually, masking is the opposite of selection; that is, masked vertices cannot be edited. However, certain vertices can be edited.

Rather, a mask is almost always removed with Ctrl + LMB and applied to the existing mask with LMB. Therefore, you will need to use the Invert operator if you want to edit the masked surfaces. If you want to mask everything that is visible, the ideal process is to clear the mask first, and then reverse it.

The A pie menu provides rapid access to both of these operators.

Face Sets

Your mesh may be rapidly concealed or exposed as previously indicated by using face sets, which arrange your mesh into distinct colored faces. They may also be utilized with the Mask Expand to quickly create masks. You may also create, modify, and join face sets with Face Set Expand.

The Alt + W pie menu contains more possibilities.

If not, the Draw Face Sets brush and Mask Gesture Tools can be used to create and modify Face Sets. The alter Face Set tool may also be used to alter them.

Auto Masking

Without needing to manually make a new mask or conceal geometry, auto-masking is another quick method of just modifying particular geometry. This function works particularly well when used in conjunction with face sets.

> **Filters**

Because they don't depend on a brush radius, filters are tools that offer an alternate method of sculpting by affecting any vertices that are visible and not masked.

You may adjust the strength by clicking and dragging from left to right. If auto-masking is enabled, the cursor's location can be utilized to selectively influence certain regions.

There are several brush kinds that are also offered as filter types. In this manner, a large portion of the mesh may be colored, smoothed, or coated with cloth simulation all at once.

> **Transforming**

In Sculpt Mode, you may also use transform tools to move, rotate, and scale, however there's a big difference from other modes. Shift-RMB may be used to manually place the pivot point in Sculpt Mode, or Mask Expand can be used to set it automatically. This guarantees that the pivot point constantly moves with the altered geometry and may be positioned more flexibly.

You can choose to always have access to the viewport gizmos by turning on the gizmos rather than always using the transform tools.

> **Painting**

Additionally, you may paint your geometry using Color Attributes like Vertex Colors in Sculpt Mode. In order to prevent needless mode switching, this makes sure that the most often performed tasks within the sculpting workflow are included in the same mode.

Painting tools may also be utilized with other sculpt mode elements like masking, filters, and face sets.

The only painting tools available in Sculpt Mode are the Paint and Smear brushes, the Color Filter, and the Mask by Color tool.

Shift is a brush that may be used for smoothing just like any other. Instead, it will blur the colors inside the brush radius while painting with brushes.

> **Adaptive Resolution**

Blender needs adequate geometry for sculpting to get results that are precise and reliable. Use one of the following adaptive sculpting techniques to add geometry dynamically, rather than beginning with a sharply split mesh.

- **Voxel Remeshing**

The geometry is rebuilt using "voxel remeshing," which creates a flawlessly even dispersed topology. This will result in a resolution that is either lower or higher depending on the specified voxel size.

This method works particularly well for obstructing an object's original form. It also has the benefit of eliminating any geometry that overlaps, which results in the creation of a manifold volume.

The remeshed output will include a re-projected mask, face sets, and color attributes that are currently in use. Depending on the hardware being utilized, large vertex counts should still be possible with this method.

- **Dyntopo**

A dynamic tessellation sculpting technique called dynamic topology (also known as Dyntopo) automatically adds and subtracts structure beneath the brush.

This allows for the creation of complicated forms without having to consider topology or resolution, in contrast to the Voxel Remesher. Additionally, it enables the definition of an alternative resolution when needed. With this method, far more intricate foundation mesh sculpting is very helpful.

This method's drawbacks include slower performance and restricted compatibility for some sculpt mode features. When utilizing Dyntopo, custom properties such as Face Sets, UV Maps, and Color properties are also lost or distorted.

When enabled, this functionality has the same shortcuts as voxel remeshing. If Constant Detail is being utilized, use Ctrl + R to flood fill the resolution after defining it with R.

- **Multi-resolution**

Subdivision-based modeling may be accomplished with the Multi-resolution Modifier. This indicates that the item will be split in a manner akin to that of the Subdivision Surface Modifier, with the exception that the subdivisions are sculptable freely for extremely fine detail.

One of the advantages of this approach is that it can be used to sculpt at any subdivision level because it can be done at numerous resolutions. This makes it possible to display lower resolutions for improved viewport efficiency while adding details at a much higher resolution for rendering and sculpting. For more extensive adjustments, it also permits sculpting at any moment at lesser resolutions.

For example, to further fix the form, you may sculpt broad proportions in subdivision level 1, add high resolution details in level 4, and then go back to subdivision 1 again.

The topology is not dynamic like voxel remeshing and dyntopo, therefore you could get certain mesh distortions as a drawback. Additionally, after a subdivision has been made, the topology shouldn't be altered because doing so will contaminate the subdivision information.

> **Cloth Sculpting**

There are several tools available right in sculpt mode that provide a more straightforward fabric Physics Simulation than manually sculpting fabric or building intricate physics simulation settings.

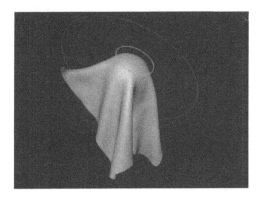

This has a number of benefits, but it's particularly helpful for creating foundation mesh and bigger apparel folds and drapes. It is feasible to detail, however the reduced fabric mechanics and slower performance on high resolution models may not provide the desired effects.

The size of the folds and the simulation's level of detail are mostly determined by the topology's resolution. Hence, it is crucial to have an ideal topology that is uniformly distributed.

Numerous sculpting features are provided; in the simulation, for instance, masked vertices are pinned. An additional illustration is the auto-masked face set bounds. The textile physics additionally applies the sculpt mode gravity factor.

The Cloth Brush and Cloth Filter are the primary brushes and tools for this functionality, however cloth sculpting may also be done with other transform brushes like Pose and Boundary by adjusting their brush parameters.

ⵜ Texture Paint

An image, sequence, or movie that is utilized to color a mesh's surface is called a UV texture. One or more UV maps are used to map the UV texture to the mesh. The picture that the UV texture uses can be determined in three different ways:

- To produce a picture, use any image editing software. Choose the UV texture and import the picture into the Image Editor. The colors will then be applied to the mesh's faces by Blender using the texture's UV map.
- Using the UV map of the presently chosen UV texture, paint a flat picture over it in the picture Editor to apply color to the mesh's faces.
- Once the model is painted in the 3D Viewport, Blender will update the UV texture using the UV map that is presently chosen (as explained below).
- Texture Paint is a built-in paint mode in Blender that's particularly made to make editing UV textures and pictures in the Image Editor or 3D Viewport quick and simple. You may use any external paint application, such as GIMP or Krita, to create a UV texture, as it is only a picture intended for a specific purpose.

A mesh may have many photos that color it since it might contain layers of UV textures. All UV textures, however, have a single picture.

Both the Image Editor and a 3D Viewport may be used with Texture Paint. By projecting into the UVs in the 3D Viewport while in Texture Paint Mode, you may paint directly on the mesh.

> **Texture preview**

You can see the effects of your painting in the context of your scene as you paint if your texture is already being used to color, bump map, displace, alpha-transparent, etc. on a model's surface in your scene (or, to put it more technically, is mapped to some aspect of a texture via a texture channel using UV as a map input).

To do this, arrange two adjacent areas: one with the Image Editor loaded and the other with the 3D Viewport's Texture Shading option selected. Set the 3D Viewport to display the UV-mapped object on the loaded picture. Known as "bump mapping," the texture being painted in the image to the right is mapped to the "Normal" property and uses a grayscale image to provide the appearance of a rough surface on a flat area. For further details on bump mapping, go to Texture Mapping Output.

> **Mask**

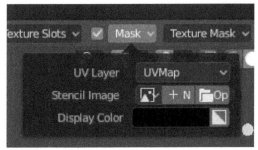

Stencil Mask

Add a texture to the image to further define masked surfaces. Painting won't alter masked surfaces, which may be specified using the Mask brush.

The header's checkbox allows you to deactivate the mask.

Cavity Mask

Cavity masking indicates, depending on the mesh choices, that the brushes will be covered if there is a hollow or a hill on the mesh surface. The algorithm used in Cavity is vertex-based.

← Vertex Painting

Vertex painting is a very easy method of painting color onto an object by directly adjusting the color of vertices instead of textures. Several render engines can use the color information that Vertex Painting maintains as a Color Attribute.

The pallette pop-over located in the center of the header allows you to adjust color attributes.

A vertex's color changes when it is painted in accordance with the brush's parameters. Following that, a gradient to the color of the other linked vertices is applied to change the color of all visible planes and edges associated to the vertex. Keep in mind that obscured faces retain their original color.

> ➤ **Editing**
- **Vertex Smooth Color**

Colors that are smooth across vertices (Paint ‣ Smooth Vertex Colors)

- **Vertex Dirty Color**

Create a gradient dirt map according to cavity (Paint ‣ Dirty Vertex Colors).

- **Vertex Color from Weight**

Converts the colors of the active weight to grayscale (Paint ‣ Vertex Color from Weight).

- **Saturation/Hue/Value**

Modify the chosen vertices' HSV values (Paint ‣ Saturation/Hue/Value).

- **Contrast and Brightness**

Modify the chosen vertices' contrast and brightness (Paint ‣ Contrast/Brightness).

✦ Weight Paint

A very high number of related vertices and, thus, a large number of weights (one weight per assigned vertex) are possible in vertex groups. One extremely natural technique to keep a lot of weight information is through Weight Painting.

The vertex groups are used to specify the relative bone impacts on the mesh, which is mostly utilized for rigging meshes. However, we also utilize it to control several modifiers, shape keys, hair density, and particle emission.

You may use the Ctrl-Tab mode option to enter Weight Paint Mode. The chosen mesh item appears in a rainbow of colors, somewhat darkened. The weights assigned to each vertex in the active vertex group are shown by the color. By default, red indicates completely weighted and blue indicates unweighted.

By using weight brushes to paint on the object, you may provide weights to its vertices. Weights are immediately added to the active vertex group when painting on a mesh (a new vertex group is established if necessary).

The pallette pop-over in the header's center allows you to control Vertex Groups.

> ➤ **The Color Code for Weighting**

A gradient with a cold/hot color scheme is used to depict weights. Low value areas, or those with weights near to 0.0, are shown as blue (cold), while high value areas, or those with weights close to 1.0, are shown as red (hot). Additionally, all intermediate values are shown as a rainbow using the hues blue, green, yellow, orange, and red.

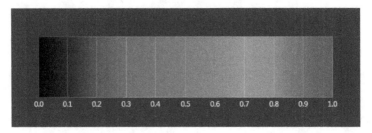

Apart from the previously mentioned color scheme, Blender offers an additional visual notation (available as an option) for unreferenced vertices, which is represented by black. As a result, you may simultaneously observe the unreferenced parts (shown in black) and the referenced areas (shown as cold/hot hues). It is most feasible to do this while searching for weighting mistakes.

- **Weight Normalized Workflow**

Weights often need to be normalized such that all deforming weights given to a single vertex total up to one in order to be utilized for things like deformation. As Blender's Armature modifier takes care of this automatically, it is theoretically not required to make sure weights are normalized before painting.

Despite being more complex, working with normalized weights has some benefits, such as enabling the use of specific tools made for this purpose and removing the need to know the weights of other groups on the same vertex in order to understand the final influence of the current group.

- ➤ **Vertex Group Uses**
- **Bones Vertex Group**

One of the primary applications of weight painting is this. Although you may have Blender produce the weights for you (see the skinning section), you might wish to adjust or even make your own, especially for areas near joints.

The steps involved are as follows:

- Using Ctrl + Tab, choose the armature and put it in Pose Mode.
- Verify that the topbar's Edit ‣ Lock Object Modes option is not selected.
- After choosing the mesh, enter Weight Paint Mode.
- Verify that the 3D Viewport's header has Bone Selection checked.
- Use Alt-LMB (or Shift-Ctrl-LMB) to choose a bone. This will cause the mesh to display the bone's current weights and activate its vertex group.
- Use LMB to paint weights for the bone.

Blender will automatically generate a vertex group for every bone that doesn't already have one when you begin painting.

You may utilize Mirror Vertex Groups to automatically construct vertex groups and weights for the other side if your armature and mesh are symmetrical.

CHAPTER 8: Grease Pencil

A Blender item is the Grease Pencil. It takes the drawing data from a pressure-sensitive or mouse stylus and projects it into three-dimensional space as a group of points called strokes.

Among other things, the Grease Pencil object may be used to create typical two-dimensional animation cut-out animation, motion graphics, and storyboards.

A new key frame for the Grease Pencil object must be added to the animation timeline in order to produce strokes in Draw Mode. Then, using Edit Mode and Sculpt Mode, existing strokes can be modified. Lastly, materials, lighting, visual effects, and modifiers may be applied to strokes by artists.

Quick Start

Artists may begin with an animated two-dimensional template or apply Grease Pencil to any pre-existing Blender scene. Some pre-configured settings are included in the template, which are useful for storyboarding and animation.

⚊ Structure

Points, edit lines, and strokes are the three primary fundamental components of the Grease Pencil object.

Points

Points are the primary component utilized in Grease Pencil object manipulation. In 3D space, a point is represented by a point.

All of the characteristics that determine how a stroke will look in the end, such as its position, thickness, alpha, weight, and UV rotation for textures, are stored in each point.

Edit Lines

While you look at a stroke in wireframe view or while you are modifying in edit mode, you will always see that points are connected by a straight line. They are utilized to create the final stroke but are not visible in the produced image.

Strokes

The displayed picture of the points and edit lines created with a certain Grease Pencil substance is called the stroke. Materials for Grease Pencil are connected at the stroke level.

⚊ Multi-Frame

You can weight paint, edit, sculpt, or draw on many frames at once using multi-frame. Very helpful for animators to avoid doing the same chore one frame at a time.

Usage

- To simultaneously sketch, edit, or sculpt, choose the relevant keyframes.
- Use the toggle button (faded lines icon) in the 3D Viewport header to activate the Multiframe tool.

- Upon activation, you are able to:
  - o Make your edits by selecting the points in each of the keyframes you've chosen.
  - o Get sculpting. All of the strokes in the chosen keyframes will be impacted by the sculpt brushes.
  - o Get painting with weights. All of the strokes in the chosen keyframes will be impacted by the weight paintbrush.
  - o Draw something now. Every keyframe that has been chosen will have the additional strokes applied to it. The Fill tool will be applied to all of the keyframes you have selected if you are using it.
  - o You can choose the stroke from the many frames in the appropriate sequence while interpolating. The selection order will be used by the interpolate tool to determine the appropriate stroke pairings.

✛ Properties
➤ Object Data
- **Grease Pencil**

To link the data across objects, utilize the Grease Pencil data-block menu.

- **2D Layers**

Strokes may be arranged into two-dimensional levels, which are unique Grease Pencil layers that aid in structuring the strokes' visibility and drawing order.

- **Onion Skinning**

Animation uses onion skinning, which allows the user to view many frames at once and make changes or judgments depending on how the previous and next frames are rendered.

➢ Layers

Every Grease Pencil object has a list of 2D layers for organizing strokes in a List view; each stroke can only be a part of a single 2D layer; new strokes are added to the active layer when you draw; by default, the layers in the viewport are arranged top to bottom.

Each layer corresponds to a channel in the Dope Sheet editor (in Grease Pencil mode); see Dope Sheet for more details.

Additionally, layers and modifiers may be used to modify certain areas of your drawing. For further details, see Modifiers.

➢ Mask Layers

There are no particular mask layers in Grease Pencil; any layer may serve as a mask for other layers. The mechanism for masking is sufficiently versatile to support both top-bottom and bottom-top masking. The layers that are used as masks can utilize any blend mode and opacity value.

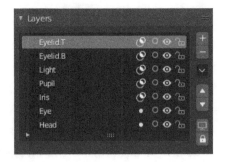

• Mask Layer List

The Mask list view may need to have the layer or layers added that will serve as the current layer's mask.

Two icon buttons that regulate the layer mask's common attributes can be found in the Masks list next to the layer name:

- **Viewports Display**

Edit Lines display parameters in both Edit and Sculpt modes.

Edit Line Color: Modifies the Edit Lines' color.

- **Canvas**

It can occasionally be challenging to determine which plane you are sketching in 3D space. A grid is displayed at the current Drawing Plane by the Canvas, a display overlay aid. The Canvas visualization is included in the Viewport Overlays.

✛ Modifiers

There are certain modifiers exclusive to Grease Pencil. Modifiers are automated processes that have a non-destructive effect on an item. Modifiers allow you to apply a variety of effects automatically without changing the underlying geometry of your object, which would otherwise be too laborious to accomplish by hand.

They function by altering an object's rendering and appearance, not its geometry, which you may alter directly. A single object can have several modifiers applied to it, creating a modifier stack. If you want to permanently alter an item, you can apply a modifier.

Grease Pencil may be modified in three different ways:

- **Modify**

These tools are comparable to the Deform ones (see below), but they often modify some other data instead of the object's shape, such vertex groups.

- **Generate**

Constructive tools that alter an object's overall look or automatically add new geometry are part of the Generate set of modifiers.

- **Deform**

The Deform set of modifiers does not introduce new geometry; instead, it only modifies an object's shape.

➢ **Generate**
- **Array Modifier**

The Array modifier makes an array of copies of the underlying object, each of which can be offset in a variety of ways from the preceding copy.

Useful for producing intricate designs that repeat.

An object may have many active array modifiers at once (e.g. to generate sophisticated three-dimensional structures).

Relative Offset

- **X, Y, Z Factor**

Adds to the offset a translation that is equal to the bounding box size of the object along each axis, multiplied by a scaling factor. Scaling factors for X, Y, and Z can be defined.

Constant Offset

- **X, Y, Z Factor**

Increments the offset of the duplicate object by a constant translation component. Constant components X, Y, and Z can be given.

Object Offset

- **X, Y, Z Distance**

Adds to the offset a transformation derived from an object (with respect to the current object). Using an empty object centered or close to the first item is best practice.

➤ **Modifier For Dot Dash**

Using the original stroke, the Dot Dash modifier creates dot dash parts.

- **Offset**

Establishes the pattern's initial offset.

- **Segment**

Constitutes a single dot dash pattern stroke.

To add or delete segments, use the plus/minus button located on the list's side.

- **Dash**

The quantity of consecutive points to be included in this section from the initial stroke.

- **Gap**

How many points are skipped after the conclusion of the section.

- **Radius**

The factor that will be applied to the radius of the original point for the new points.

- **Opacity**

The opacity factor for the new points that should be applied to the original point.

- **Material Index**

For produced segments, use this index; for existing stuff, use -1.

- **Use Cyclic**

End the section.

➢ **Envelop Modifier**

The envelope modifier joins all of those points with n points between them by creating an envelope shape over the current strokes.

➢ **Line Modifier**

Stylized line art is produced by the Line Art modifier from a scene, set, or item.

There must be an active camera in the scene for the modifier's effects to be seen. The lines that are formed are limited to the areas of the item that are visible to this camera.

Geometry Processing

- **Personalized Camera**

To calculate strokes, use the custom camera rather than the active camera. Useful for motion graphic effects and for baking several shots from various perspectives.

- **Crossing Edges as Curvature**

This option enables the drawing of overlapping edges as contours, such as those from imported geometry or an Edge Split modifier when two edges occupy the exact same region. If this option is enabled, the computation will be significantly slower, but edge overlapping instances will be handled without producing incorrect occlusion results.

- **Objects that are Instanced**

The loading of particles and other instanced objects for line art computation is made possible by this option. When there are several instanced objects in the scene, performance will be affected.

- **Cutting Off Boundaries**

When this option is selected, line art will produce contour-style clipping lines whenever the model is cut by close or distant clipping planes. There won't be any queues otherwise.

Bake

- **Bake Line Art**

Bakes Line Art strokes in the start and finish frame range of the scene for the current Grease Pencil item. All Grease Pencil objects with at least one Line Art modifier are baked when you use the Bake Line Art (All) command. Baked Line Art modifications will automatically deactivate after baking.

- **Cleared Bake Line Art**

Releases the active Grease Pencil object from baked line art frames that are inside the scene frame range. All Grease Pencil objects with at least one Line Art modifier are subject to the same process when using Clear Baked Line Art (All).

➢ **Mirror Modifier**

The strokes are mirrored across the Object Origin along the local X, Y, and/or Z axes using the Mirror modifier. It can also employ the local axes of that item rather than its own by using it as the mirror center and then using those axes.

- **Axis**

The direction adjacent to the mirror planes of symmetry is known as the X, Y, Z axis, and this is the axis along which to mirror.

When you mirror an object on the X plane, the positive X value from the original stroke become the negative X value on the mirrored side. This illustrates how the axis relates to the mirror direction.

There are several axes available for selection. After which more mirrored copies will be obtained. Eight mirrors are obtained with all three axes, four mirrors with two axes, and one mirror with one axis.

- **Object**

A data ID to designate an item, normally empty, whose rotation and position will generate mirror planes instead of utilizing the updated object's coordinates.

> **Simplify Modifier**

By using the Simplify modifier, you may make the strokes have fewer points. This modification seeks to minimize points while preserving the geometry of the lines.

Using the modifier during animation can improve performance (more frames per second).

⊥ **Deform**

> **Armature Modifier**

Characters and other objects that require posing may be animated by creating skeletal systems using the Armature Modifier.

An object may be precisely molded by adding an armature, eliminating the need for manual geometry animation.

> **Hook Modifier**

The Hook Modifier is a tool for deforming stroke points with the help of another item—any object will do, but it's often empty or a bone.

The hook extracts points from the strokes as it advances. Consider it to be a form of dynamic proportional editing.

> ➤ **Noise Modifier**

By adding a variety of values that cause the line to become unstable and noisy, the Noise Modifier modifies the value of one or more stroke/point parameters, such as location, strength, thickness, or UV texture position.

For more striking effects, the noise component might have random values.

> ✦ **Shrinkwrap**

A Grease Pencil item can "shrink" to the surface of another object by using the Shrinkwrap modifier. Every point of the item being changed is moved to the location that is closest to it on the specified mesh's surface.

> • **Wrap Method**

This choice sets which algorithm will be applied to each point of the changed item to find the closest point on the target's surface. Certain settings will augment the panel with additional, specialized controls. For a description of each technique, see Wrap Methods.

- **Snap Mode**

To adjust how the point is transported to the destination point chosen by the previously mentioned techniques, most modes offer an extra parameter. Only when Offset is non-zero do some of the options alter.

Above the surface: There is always a shift in the point. In order to return to the original location, the offset is applied along the projection line that joins the original point and the chosen destination point.

Inside: If the point is inside the target already, it is not moved. Along the projection line, offset reduces the permitted volume in the direction of the interior.

Outside: If the point is outside the target, it stays there. Along the projection line, offset enlarges the exclusion volume outside.

External Surface: Similar to On Surface, however the offset is always placed outside of the intended area.

Above the Surface: Similar to On Surface, except with the offset applied along the target's smooth normal.

✛ Materials

The Grease Pencil object's appearance is determined by its materials. They specify the strokes' primary color as well as the filled regions' texture.

The selected material is the sole active item in the list at all times. The active substance is used in fresh strokes when you draw.

Using the tools in Vertex Mode or the Draw and Tint tool in Draw Mode, you may change the color of the basic material.

Since the substance and the strokes are inextricably related, any alteration to one will affect how previously drawn strokes appear.

> ➤ **Grease Pencil Shader**

A Grease Pencil object's filled regions and/or strokes can be worked with using the Grease Pencil shader.

A checkbox on the panel header allows you to enable the stroke and fill components, which have their own section panel.

Only the lines are affected by stroke, and only the regions defined by closed lines—those formed by joining the start and end points of the lines—are affected by fill.

> ➤ **Setting Up Materials**

Materials for grease pencils may be produced in Blender's Material properties just like any other material. For further details, see to Material assignment.

To interactively preview how the material appears in the scene, the 3D Viewport may be changed to either Material Preview or Rendered shading.

Materials for Grease Pencils are data-blocks that may be linked to one or more objects. Moreover, distinct materials can be linked to distinct strokes.

The material and brush options in Grease Pencil determine how the final strokes will feel and look.

Additional options for working with materials while drawing or altering lines are now available in the Materials slots of the List view.

⤏ Draw Mode

Grease Pencil has a setting called sketch setting that lets you sketch in the 3D Viewport. Actually, the only mode where new strokes may be made is this one.

Draw Mode does not allow you to pick previously created strokes; instead, you must use the alter or Sculpt modes to alter strokes.

CHAPTER 9: Rigging and Animation

⤏ Animation

An object can be animated to move or change shape over time. There are several techniques to animate an object:

> ➤ **Moving as a whole entity**

- Deforming them:

Changing their size, orientation, or location over time bringing their control points or vertices to life;

- Inherited animation:

Causing an item to move in response to another object's movement (such as its parent, hook, armature, etc.).

⤏ Rigging

The broad word for attaching controls to an object, usually for animation, is rigging.

When rigging, one or more of the following aspects are frequently used:

- Your rig may therefore manage many values at once and set some attributes to update automatically in response to changes made elsewhere.

- The complexity of rigging may be tailored to your project; animators can focus on creating their own user interfaces rather than worrying about the fundamental workings of the rig.
- For character animation, an armature and modifier are frequently utilized to distort a mesh.
- To imitate real-world camera rigs, a camera rig may be utilized in place of animating the camera object directly (e.g., effects like camera jitter can be applied using a boom arm positioned on a revolving pedestal).

↓ Keyframe

All a keyframe is a time marker that holds a property's value.
For instance, a keyframe may specify that, on frame 1, a cube's horizontal position is at 3 m.

A keyframe is meant to enable interpolated animation. For instance, the user could add a key on frame 10 to specify the cube's horizontal position at 20 meters. Depending on the interpolation method (e.g., Linear, Bézier, Quadratic, etc.) chosen, Blender would then automatically determine the cube's correct position for all the frames between frame 1 and 10.
The Dope Sheet editor provides a summary of all the keyframes that are currently in use.

• Visualization

Animation may benefit from a few key visualization capabilities in the 3D Viewport.

The name of this object (displayed in the top left corner of the 3D Viewport) becomes yellow when the current frame is a keyframe for the currently active item.

- **Interpolation**

The representation and management of keyframe interpolation is done via animation curves, or F-Curves. The Graph Editor allows you to see and edit these curves. Time is represented by the X axis of the curve, while the property's value is shown by the Y axis. The curve's points are defined by the keyframes itself, with extra parameters controlling the interpolation process.

The primary option that controls how the curve is interpolated from one keyframe to the next for each keyframe is called the Interpolation Mode. In addition to a free form Bézier mode, there are other modes with fixed forms, such as constant, linear, quadratic, etc.

The curve's extrapolation indicates how far it stretches before and after the initial and ending keyframes. Constant and Linear are the two primary options; the curve can also be set up to loop.

Handles, that have a handle type and location, govern Bézier interpolation. While Vector, Automatic, and Auto Clamped handles are automatically derived from keyframe values, Free and Aligned handle positions must be explicitly adjusted using the Graph editor.

The per-curve Auto Handle Smoothing techniques option determines how the three automated handle types are calculated. The None mode just takes the values of the keys that are directly adjacent to each other, much to how most other software functions. While the Continuous Acceleration option delivers better results right out of the box, it also has a tendency to overshoot more when using Automatic handles. This is because changes in one key effect interpolation over a greater area of the curve.

⁂ Editing
➤ Keyframe Inserting

Adding new keys may be done in a few different ways. Specifically:

- I will key properties in the 3D Viewport according to the User Preferences for Default Key Channels.
- Reading the User Preferences is not done while a Keying Set is active.
- You may use the context menu by right-clicking on a property and selecting Insert Keyframe, or you can use the mouse to hover over a property and hit I.
- Holding down the I key while dragging the mouse will display a pie menu where you may input Location, Rotation, Scale, and Available if the User Preference "Pie Menu on Drag" is enabled.

➤ Auto Keyframe

The Timeline header's record button is called Auto Keyframe. When the value for a transform type property changes, Auto Keyframe automatically inserts keyframes to the specified frame.

Keyframe Animation
You can see how to animate a cube's position, rotation, and scale by looking at this example.

- First, set the frame to one in the Timeline or other animation editors.

- In Object Mode, pick the cube and hit I in the 3D Viewport. This will log the cube's position, rotation, and scale on frame 1.
- A 100 frame rate should be used.
- To change the cube, use Move G, Rotate R, and Scale S.
- In the 3D Viewport, press I.

Use the Spacebar to start the animation and test it out.

> **Keying Sets**

A group of animated properties called keying sets are used to keyframe and animate several attributes at once. In the 3D Viewport, for instance, hitting K will display the various Keying Sets. After that, Blender will create keyframes for the selected Keying Set. Both bespoke Keying Sets termed "Absolute Keying Sets" and certain pre-installed Keying Sets are available.

- **Adding Properties to a Keying Set**

A few methods for giving Keying Sets properties.

Choose Add Single to Keying Set or Add All to Keying Set after right-clicking on the property in the User Interface. In the event that no Keying Set is currently in use, this will add the attributes to the one that is.
Press K after moving the mouse pointer over the properties to add all to Keying Set.

- **Set active Keying set**

There are many methods for identifying the active keying set:
- In the 3D Viewport, hit Shift-K.
- With the Keying Set panel open, select a keying set.

- Using the Keyed popover within the Timeline header, choose a keying set.

- **Whole Character keying Set**

All of the characteristics in a character rig that are likely to be animated are keyframed using the integrated Whole Character Keying Set. The Old Pose Library system also made use of it subtly.

Bones whose names begin with one of the following prefixes are ignored by this keying set because it believes they are technical bones that are not intended for direct animation. For example, these bones are generated with the integrated Rigify plugin.

- COR (Corrective)
- DEF (Deformation)
- GEO (Geometry)
- MCH (Mechanism)
- ORG (Original from meta rig)
- VIS (Visualization)

⊥ Lattice

Lattice: Outside of Blender, also known as deformation cage. A lattice is made up of a grid of vertices that is non-renderable in three dimensions. Its primary function is to employ a Lattice Modifier to apply an alteration to the item it controls. When an item has Lattice Deform as its parent, a Lattice Modifier is added automatically.

➢ Usage

In item Mode, the lattice has to be adjusted in size and position to accommodate your item. The item will distort if any scaling is performed while it is in edit mode. This includes using Ctrl-A to apply its scale, which will have the same effect as scaling the lattice in Edit Mode and, consequently, the object.

➢ Constraints

With constraints, you may manipulate an object's attributes (such its position, rotation, and scale) by either utilizing a target object (like the "copy" ones) or only static values (like the "limit" ones).

Constraints are helpful in static projects as well, but animation is clearly where they are most effective.

Through the targets that its limitations employ, you may direct the animation of an object (indirect animation). As a result, animating the targets will also indirectly animate the owner of the constraint as these targets can then change the owner's attributes.

The restrictions' settings are animateable. For example, the Influence or, when utilizing the bone of an armature as the target, animate the area between the root and tip of the bone where the actual target point is located.

They can let a dinosaur's legs bend at the knee automatically, enable a bus's wheels to revolve in unison, enable a tennis player's eyes to track a tennis ball bouncing across the court, and make it simple for a hand to grasp a sword's hilt and swing the weapon with the hand. In Blender, constraints interact with bones and objects.

➤ Including and Excluding Constraint

Click the Add Object Constraint option in the Constraints tab to add a constraint. An alternative is to use the operator Add Constraint (with Targets).

Use Copy Constraints to Selected Objects to copy constraints from one object to another.

The "X" button located in the constraint's header can be used to eliminate any one constraint. Use Clear Object Constraints to remove all constants from an object.

➤ Tips

A great method to add complexity and intricacy to a rig is via constraints.

However, use caution to avoid jumping in headfirst and adding restrictions after restrictions until you completely lose understanding of how they work together.

Begin easily. Learn every detail about a single limitation. A useful constraint to start with is the Copy Location Constraint, which also includes an example of animation. The other limitations will make much more sense if you take the time to comprehend every underlying idea.

➤ Header

A header exists for each restriction. The following explanation of the header's interface parts uses a Copy Location restriction as an example.

↓ Common

➢ Target

You may associate the constraint with any Target object by filling in the Target Data ID field. For the constraint to start working, this link supplies data. For instance, location information is required for the Copy Location Constraint to work. Once the Target field is filled in, the Copy Location constraint will start using the Target object's location information.

The Object Origin will be used as the target location by default by the Target.

A Vertex Group field will show up if the Target field refers to a Mesh or Lattice object. If you enter the name of a vertex group, the object's origin will not be the constraint's target; rather, it will be the vertex group's median point.

A Head/Tail slider and a Bone field will show up if the Target field ties to a Armature. If you enter the name of a bone, the constraint will target the bone itself, rather than the origin of the armature object as a whole.

The target's exact location is moved via the slider between the bone's head and tail. Certain limitations provide a button next to the slider that makes it possible to use Bendy Bones' curved form.

➢ Space

For constraints to work, they require a frame of reference. The "space" of the constraint is the name given to this frame of reference. Selecting one space over another will modify this framework and significantly impact a constraint's behavior.

Try experimenting with two empties to see how altering the space affects the constraint's behavior. Ensure that they appear as arrows so that you can view each empty's local axis. To ensure that they are always visible, even when stacked on top of one another, be sure to make one empty slightly bigger than the other. After that, add a constraint on one empty that targets the other, and do extensive experimentation by varying the target's position, rotation, and scale.

- Owner Space and Target Space

The Target space is the place that is utilized to assess the constraint's target. The Owner space is the space that is utilized to assess the constrained item, or the object that is the owner of the constraint. To find out if a space selection impacts the target's space or the owner's space, hover over the relevant space select menu.

There won't be any, one, or two selectors when the restrictions make use of a Target and/or/and/or an Owner space. In this example, the Copy Location restriction uses both the Owner and Target spaces.

The Target and Owner spaces in a constraint can be a variety of space types when they are used together.

➢ **Space Type**

- **World Space**

The object's (or bone's) frame of reference in this form of space is the world. The place is in relation to its global origin. The world axes are the orientation of both rotation and scale.

Considerations include modifications made to the object, the object's parent, and any additional constraints that are positioned higher in the constraint stack.

- **Local Space**

This space does not include the orientation and rest position of the bone itself, nor any impacts from the parent objects or bones. Only those changes that are applied to the bone or object itself are considered.

- **Bones only (Local with Parent)**

The orientation and position of the bone are assessed in reference to their rest posture, taking into account both their own transformations and those that may result from a potential parent relationship (i.e., the transformations of the chain above the bone).

- **Pose Space (Bones only)**

The evaluation of the bone's location and orientation takes place in the local space of the armature, separate from the armature modifications in Object Mode. Thus, Pose Space and World Space will both have the same effect if the armature object contains null transformations.

- **Custom Space**

When this option is chosen, extra input fields appear with the purpose of allowing the position and orientation to be assessed in relation to the present location and orientation of an arbitrary object or bone. This allows the constraint to be evaluated using any coordinate system.

- **Owner Orientation (Local Space Bones Target only)**

With an extra coordinate space transformation to account for the different rest posture orientations of the target and owner bones, this space functions similarly to Local Space. As long as the parents are still in the resting position, applying this as the owner's local space will result in the same global space movement as the target.

⁜ Stack

The restrictions Stack is the totality of all the restrictions that have an impact on an item. Under the Add Constraint menu in the Constraints panel is where you'll find the Stack.

The stack's constraints are assessed top to bottom. The ultimate result of the stack is significantly influenced by the sequence in which each restriction is applied. The behavior of the entire stack may be altered by rearranging the restrictions.

➢ Constraint Camera Solver

The location and rotation of the "solved camera motion" are provided to the constraint owner by the Camera Solver constraint.

With "solved camera motion," Blender reconstructs the actual camera's location with relation to the object being tracked at the time the video was recorded.

➢ Actions

Actions capture and hold the data while animating properties and objects in Blender. Actions are data-blocks in Blender, same as anything else.

Therefore, the animation is stored to the Action when you use keyframes to animate an object by altering its position.

Every property, like Cube. location, has a channel to which it is recorded. Channel X Location is where x is recorded. If all objects have X location and Y location attributes below them, then the X location and Y location properties can be shared by numerous objects.

> ➤ **Working with Action**

Blender produces an Action to capture the data when you animate an object for the first time by adding keyframes.

The Sidebar area of the NLA Editor or the Action data-block option in the Dope Sheet Action Editor header can be used to handle actions.

Press the shield button after each action if you are doing numerous actions for the same object. This will make Blender save the unlinked activities and assign the actions a Fake User.

Only one Action may be edited by an object at a time. You may combine numerous actions using the NLA Editor.

- **Properties**

When a channel or NLA track is chosen, a panel that appears in the Dope Sheet or the NLA Editor may be used to manually set the intended usable frame range of an action.

Manual Frame Range

Manually define the action's desired playback frame range (some tools utilize this range, but it has no bearing on animation assessment). The checkbox has the ability to toggle the manual frame range capability.

The range is utilized for creating a new track based on the action to NLA, rather than the actual range filled by key frames. Exporters can use it to decide which range of frames to export as well.

To differentiate it from a solid fill for the present playback range, the range is shown as diagonal hash fill in the editor's backdrop.

While fractional values are possible, integer values are often anticipated for the frame values.

Cyclic Animation

Indicates that a cycle within the given range is the anticipated behavior of the activity. The range should contain the duplicated start key of the loop, meaning that the first and end frames should depict the identical stance of the cycle one loop apart.

⊥ Driver

Drivers are a manner of using a function, or mathematical expression, to control property values.

In practical terms, drivers include:

- A driver configuration that uses custom Python expressions or other attributes to provide zero, one, or more input values, which are then combined using a predetermined mathematical formula.
- A F-Curve animation that converts the driver configuration's output to the ultimate value that will be applied to the driven property.

- For instance, the size of Object 2 can regulate the rotation of Object 1. The rotation of Object 1 is therefore said to be driven by the scale of Object 2.

In addition to setting a property's value to another value directly, drivers may also combine several values using a fixed function or a Python expression, and then further modify it using a modifier stack, a manually specified curve, or both.

Typically used to drive bone transformations and the impact of shape keys, action restrictions, and modifiers, drivers are incredibly useful tools for designing rigs. They frequently employ custom attributes as inputs.

➢ **Graph View**

An F-Curve representing the driver function is displayed in the Drivers editor's main section. The driver configuration's output value is mapped into the X axis. The configuration affects the units.

The value applied to the target property is displayed on the Y axis. The property determines the units.

➢ **Configuring Driver**

The driver setup is displayed in the Drivers panel.

There can be none, one, or many variables for a driver. The attributes, object transformation channels, and relative distances between objects that the driver uses as inputs are specified by variables.

The way the variables are utilized depends on the type of driver. The kind might be:

- An integrated function, such as the total of the variables' values, or
- An arbitrary Python expression that refers to the variables by name is called a programmed expression.

A single value is produced by this driver setup, and it changes when the variables do. The result to be applied to the driven property is then obtained by evaluating this value through the driver function curve.

➤ Usage

Drivers can be added to properties by putting an expression directly into the property's value, using their context menu, a shortcut, or copy-pasting.

Once drivers have been added, they are often edited using the Drivers editor or a condensed Edit Driver popover that may be accessed via the property context menu.

• Add Driver

Adding a driver to a property is often done by RMB Select Add Driver from the context menu after clicking a property. Moreover, drivers may be added by moving the mouse pointer over the property and pressing Ctrl-D.

This adds a driver and shows the Edit Driver popover. The driver has only one variable, which has to be filled up.

• Edit Driver

Opens a popover window that lets you change the driver's input variables and custom expression without opening the complete Drivers Editor.

This condensed interface is adequate because a lot of drivers don't use their F-Curve component.

- **Open Editors for Driver**

Chooses the driver connected to the property by opening a new window containing the Drivers Editor.

- **Copy and Paste**

Through the context menu, drivers may be copied and pasted. This can save time adjusting settings when adding drivers with the same configurations.

- **Copy as a new Driver**

With the Copy As New Driver dialog option of the input property, one may rapidly construct a driver that changes the property value to a separate property. The driver can then be pasted into the output property using Paste Driver.

Alternatively, you may use the editor panel's Paste Driver Variables button to add the new driver variable to an already-existing driver.

➢ **Markers**

In an animation, markers are used to identify frames that include important details or noteworthy occurrences. For instance, the camera may move, a door may open, or a character's motion may begin. It is possible to give markers names to make them more instantly understood. Many of Blender's editors have them accessible.

The following editors are capable of creating and editing markers:
- Graph Editor

- Dope Chart
- Editor NLA
- Editor for Video Sequences
- Timetable

- **Types**

Pose markers are a different kind of marker that are exclusive to armatures and shape keys, in addition to ordinary markers. They serve as posture indicators in Dope Sheet's Actions Editor phase and Shape Keys Editor.

- **Standard**

Regular markers appear as tiny white triangles with a dashed line covering the editor height at the relevant frame, and are empty or filled when chosen. If they have a name, it is displayed in white to the right of them.

- **3d Viewport**

Although you cannot add, update, or delete markers using the 3D Viewport, you can see their name when on their frame in the top left corner of the Object Info window.

- **Pose Markers**

In the Dope Sheet, pose markers are shown by a diamond-shaped symbol. Pose markers appear as a red dashed line inside the relative action strip in the NLA editor.

- **Bind Camera to Markers**

The unique operator Bind Camera to Markers is exclusive to the Timeline. The operator enables the active object to be configured as the active camera by using markers.

Choose the item you want to be the active camera and a marker to link the active camera to in order to utilize this operator. When the operator is used, a marker will be added if none is selected. A marker that has an object tied to it will have its name changed to reflect the name of the current object. To set them apart from other educational markers, these markers additionally have a camera symbol to the left of the name.

You can reposition these markers to alter the frame at which the marker's bound item becomes the active camera.

- **Motion Path**

You may see how points move over a sequence of frames as routes with the Motion routes tool. Bone joints and item origins are examples of these points.

The bones must be chosen before motion routes may be added or removed. Next:
- To display the pathways or make necessary updates, use the Calculate Path button.
- Click the Clear routes button to make the routes invisible.

For unselected locations on the pathways, a light gray color is displayed; for chosen points, a slightly bluish gray color is displayed. The direction of travel is indicated by a glow surrounding the current frame, which is blue for frames ahead and green for frames behind. On the pathways, a little white dot represents each frame.

The routes are active throughout animation playback and are immediately updated when you modify your postures or keyframes. Only when utilizing the Around Frame type does playing the animation have an impact on the pathways.

⊹ Path Types

The range that Motion Paths should display.

Around the Frame: Show the points' trajectories around the current frame for a predetermined number of frames. This button provides pathways for a specified number of frames before to and after the current frame.

In Range: Show the routes of the points inside the given range.

CHAPTER 10: Physics

The physics framework in Blender lets you model a variety of real-world physical events. These systems may be used to produce a wide range of static and dynamic effects, including:

-
  Flocks, grass, and hair
- Rainfall
- Dust and smoke

- Water
- Cloth
- Jelly etc.

＋ Rigid Body

Solid object motion may be simulated using the rigid body simulation. It does not distort objects; instead, it modifies their position and orientation.

The stiff body simulation in Blender interfaces more closely with the animation system than the other simulations. Rigid bodies may therefore be utilized in parent-child relationships, animation restrictions, and drivers just like ordinary objects.

➤ Creating a Rigid Body

A rigid body simulation can only contain mesh objects. Object ‣ Rigid Body menu − Add Active/Add Passive to build rigid bodies, utilize the Rigid Body button located in the Physics tab of the Properties.

Rigid bodies can be classified as either active or passive. Whereas passive bodies stay still, active bodies are dynamically simulated. When selecting the animated option, the animation system may control both kinds.

The orientation and location of dynamic rigid body objects will be superseded by the rigid body system during the simulation. However, take note that the objects' rotation and placement remain unchanged, making the rigid body simulation function more like a restriction. Use the implement Object Transform operator to implement the rigid body transformations.

Although it is always under the direction of the animation system, the rigid body object's scale also affects the simulation.

The Rigid Body button on the Physics tab of the Properties or the Object ▸ Rigid Body option may be used to remove the object's rigid body physics.

➢ Working with Rigid Body

There are a number of object operators available for handling stiff bodies; these operators are accessible through the stiff Body object menu. These operators contain functions to apply rigid body constraints, change the attributes of rigid bodies, and add and delete rigid bodies.

• Rigid Body World

A collection of rigid body objects known as the Rigid Body World contains configurations common to all the rigid bodies in this model.

Upon applying rigid body physics to an item, a set of objects named "Rigid Body World" is automatically formed. When rigid body to this group. Using the Collections panel, you may distribute the physics is applied to an item, it automatically adds the object stiff body objects and build many stiff Body World Collections. ⸝

The simulation only considers rigid body objects and restrictions that are present in the collection that is defined in the Collections field of the panel of Rigid Body World in the Scene tab.

➢ Rigid Body Constraint

Rigid body joints, sometimes called constraints, unite two rigid bodies. It is intended for the physics restrictions to be affixed to an empty object. The two physics-enabled objects that the constraint will bind have fields that can be directed at by the constraint. Unlike the two constrained items, the empty object gives the constraint a position and an axis. On each of the two constrained objects, the position of the entity holding the physics constraint indicates a set of axes and a location. The location and orientation of these two anchor points, which are determined at the start of the animation, are fixed in the object's local coordinate system for the length of the animation. Although the objects are free to move away from the constraint object, the constraint anchor follows the object's path. Consider employing numerous objects with a non-physics Child of restriction and animating the child's relative placement if this feature appears restrictive.

⊹ Physics Menu

Additionally, you may use the Rigid Body Constraint button on the Physics tab in the Properties to create a rigid body constraint on any of the two constrained objects. The placement and rotation of the item upon which this restriction was established are factors that influence it. In this manner, no empty objects are produced for the constraint. This object takes on the function of the empty object. To improve constraint driving, the constrained object might then be set to a passive type.

Further settings show up in the Properties of the selected empty object or one of the two constrained objects with the constructed constraint in the panel of the Rigid Body Constraint of the Physics tab.

➢ Types of Constraint

- **Fixed**

The two things move together as a result of this limitation. The objects do not move with the same rigidity as they would if they were all part of the same mesh since the physics system does contain a little amount of slop.

- **Point**

A point bearing connects the objects, permitting any rotation around the constraint object's position, but not relative translation. The physics engine will attempt to ensure that the two points on the two constrained objects that are indicated by the constraint object coincide.

- **Hinge**

Between two objects, the hinge allows for one degree of flexibility. There are strict limitations on translation. The object housing the Physics constraint (often an Empty, separate from the two objects being connected) may rotate along its Z axis. You may control the hinge's axis and anchor by varying the rotation and location of the object housing the constraint.

The Z axis is used instead of the X axis by the Hinge, which is the unique single-axis rotating restriction. Examine your other limitations to determine whether they might be the source of the issue if your hinge isn't working properly.

- **Slider**

Although relative rotation and translation along other axes are not permitted, the Slider constraint does permit relative translation along the constraint object's X axis.

- **Piston**

A piston permits translation along the X axis of the constraint object. It also allows rotation around the X axis of the constraint object. It is like a combination of the freedoms of a slider with the freedoms of a hinge (neither of which is very free alone).

- **Generic**

Numerous parameters are available for the generic constraint.

You may restrict the quantity of translation across the objects by using the constraints on the X, Y, and Z axes. The same outcome as the point constraint is achieved by clamping the min/max to zero.

The objects remain aligned when the relative rotation is clamped to zero. The behavior of combining a translation clamp with an absolute rotation would resemble that of the Fixed constraint.

Any parameter that has a nonzero spread applied to it will fluctuate in that range during the simulation.

- **Generic Spring**

To all the choices accessible on the Generic constraint, the generic spring constraint adds certain spring parameters for the X, Y, and Z axes. When the spring is used alone, the items move as though they are attached to the constraining object by a spring that is fastened there. For most purposes, this is a bit too much flexibility, and it is best to enable translation or rotation limitations.

Unusual behavior results from the spring pressures being unable to realign the anchor points when the dampening on the springs is set to 1. Check the damping if your springs are behaving strangely.

- **Motor**

Two entities are translated and/or rotated as a result of the motor constraint. Two things can be driven together or apart by it. It can drive translation and basic rotation, but unlike a screw, it won't be restricted since other physical laws can limit translation without affecting rotation.

The object housing the constraint's X axis serves as the rotation axis. The Hinge, on the other hand, employs the Z axis. It is especially important to align the axes since the Motor is susceptible to confounding disturbances in the absence of a corresponding Hinge constraint. The motor will appear to have no impact if it is not properly aligned because the hinge is impeding the motor's action.

- **Tips**

The Animated checkbox on the Rigid Body panel on the Physics header in the Properties should be closely inspected, just as with any other physics-enabled object. Not ticking the Animated box while using the keyframe animation for an inactive physics object is a typical error. Disappointment will result from the item moving but the physics engine acting as though the Passive is still in its initial position.

Animation

The most popular method is to keyframe animate both the animated checkbox and the position or spin of an Active physics object. The object's rotation, velocity, and last known position are used by the physics engine to assume control when a curve within the animated property changes to disabled.

Animating the strengths of different factors (such the limits of a hinge, the target velocity of a motor, etc.) may provide a broad range of intriguing outcomes.

When a constraint is enabled during a physics simulation, it frequently produces dramatic outcomes since the physics engine is trying to align two objects that are frequently far out of alignment. The impacted items frequently accumulate enough kinetic energy to bounce out of the frame.

Using the Bake to Keyframes option under the Object ▸ Rigid Body menu, rigid body dynamics may be baked to standard keyframes.

> **Simulation Stability**

Steps per second may be increased to improve simulation stability in the simplest method possible. Care must be used though, since creating an excessive number of steps might lead to issues and further reduce the stability of the simulation (if you require more than 1000 steps, you should consider other options to increase stability).

Extending the amount of solver iterations contributes to improving object stacking stability and strengthening restrictions.

Small things should be avoided as they are unstable right now. Objects should ideally have a diameter of at least 20 cm. Setting the collision margin to 0 is typically not advised, however it can help make little objects behave more naturally if it is still required.

Objects can pass through one another when they are tiny or move quickly. In addition to the previously indicated advice, in this instance it is best to avoid employing mesh forms. Because mesh forms are made up of individual triangles rather than having any true thickness, things may pass through them more readily. You may increase the collision margin to give them some thickness.

⊹ Cloth

One of the most difficult parts of computer graphics is simulating cloth, an object that appears straightforward and is often taken for granted in reality but actually involves a lot of intricate internal and external relationships. Typically, 2D mesh is used to represent cloth in order to replicate real-world items like banners, flags, and textiles. However, fabric may also be used to simulate 3D things like balls, cushions, balloons, and teddy bears.

You have control over how cloth interacts with and is impacted by other moving objects, the wind, and other factors, in addition to a generic aerodynamic model.

A Cloth Modification will be assigned to the object's modifier stack after cloth physics has been applied to a mesh. It can therefore react with other modifiers like Armature and Smooth in its capacity as a modifier. Under these circumstances, the final mesh form is calculated based on the modifier stack order. For instance, when the modifier computes the cloth's form, you should smooth the material.

To lock in or freeze the mesh's form at that frame, apply the Cloth Modifier. This removes the modifier. For instance, you might cover a table with a flat cloth, run the simulation, and then add the modification. You are essentially saving yourself by utilizing the simulator in this way.

The simulation's output is cached, saving the mesh's form from having to be computed again after it has already been determined for a particular animation frame. You are in complete control of wiping the cache and starting the experiment again if you make modifications to the simulation. The first time the simulation runs, it does so automatically with no baking or additional steps interfering with the process.

Because the cloth's form is automatically calculated at each frame and is done in the background, you may carry on with your job while the simulation runs. It is, however, CPU-intensive, and the amount of CPU required to compute the mesh varies, as does the possible lag, depending on your PC's capability and the intricacy of the simulation.

- **Workflow**

When dealing with cloth, a common procedure is to:
- Use the Cloth object as a basic form to begin with.
- In the Properties, under the Physics tab, label the item as "cloth."
- Model additional deflection elements that will come into contact with the cloth. Make sure that the Deflection modification comes after any other mesh-deforming modifiers in the modifier stack.
- Illuminate the cloth, apply materials and textures, and, if preferred, do UV unwrapping.
- Give the thing some particles, like steam rising from the surface, if you'd like.
- Run the simulation and make the necessary adjustments to get the desired outcomes. For this phase, the Timeline editor's playback controls work really well.

- To acquire a new default beginning form, you can choose to age the mesh to a certain point throughout the simulation.
- To fix small tears in the mesh, make little adjustments frame by frame.
-

± Fluid

➤ Liquid Simulations

The physical characteristics of liquids, particularly water, are simulated using fluid physics. It is possible to label certain items in Blender to be included in the flowing simulation while building a scene. A domain that delineates the area that the simulation occupies is necessary for a fluid simulation. You may specify the global parameters for simulation (gravity and viscosity, for example) under the domain settings.

➤ Gas Simulations

Within the scope of the fluids system, gas or smoke simulations may be used to simulate mixtures of gases, liquid particles, and solids in the air, including smoke. In addition to creating dynamic Voxel textures that may be used for rendering, it mimics the fluid movement of air and represents the density, heat, and velocity of various other fluids or suspended particles, such as smoke.

Within a Domain, a mesh object or particles system releases smoke or gases. The airflow in the domain, which is impacted by Effector objects, governs the passage of smoke. The force fields and gravity in the setting will also have an impact on smoke. Via the Fluid Flow force field, airflow in the domain can influence other physics models.

- **Settings**

The complete simulation is included in the domain object. Fluid simulations are not allowed to exit the domain; based on the parameters, they will either vanish or crash against the edge.

Remember that larger domains require longer bake times and higher resolutions. It should be just big enough for the simulation to fit inside it, without being so big that it takes too long to calculate.

Add a cube and move it about until it completely encloses the region wherein you'd like the simulation to happen to establish a domain. Scaling, rotation, and translation are all permitted. Select Fluid in the Properties ‣ Physics tab and choose Domain as the fluid type to make it a fluid domain.

> **Flow**

In order to add or remove fluid from a domain object, utilize fluid flow types. For a flow object to function, it must be enclosed within the domain's Bounding Box.

Click Fluid in Properties ‣ Physics to apply Fluid physics to any mesh object and specify it as a Flow object. Next, choose Flow as the kind of fluid. A predefined fluid flow origin object should now be available to you.

CHAPTER 11: Video Editing

Blender is useful not just for modeling and animation but also for video editing. There are two viable approaches to this: the Video Sequencer, which is covered in this chapter, and the Compositor. Blender's Video Sequencer is a comprehensive video editing system that lets you mix and match different video channels as well as add effects to them. When combined with Blender's animation capabilities, these effects may be used to make impactful video cuts!

⬥ Directory Structure

Most often, a video production combines a number of distinct elements. They may be divided into three main groups.

- Video files include images, graphic files (logos, charts, etc.), video clips (or movies in Blender lingo), and Visual Effects (VFX) including masks, lens flares, and animation.
- Audio files include voice-over, music, recorded dialogue, and Sound Effects (SFX) like swooshes and ambient noises.
- Project files include mix files, backups, render results (partial), and scripts and storyboards for documentation.

Edit Your Project

There isn't a single best practice for editing videos that works for all situations. There are undoubtedly various specialized use cases, such as video instructional editing and wedding film production, but there is general consensus regarding the separation of four fundamental tasks.

➤ Montage

Montage is the process of putting disparate clips—text, audio, video, and effects—together into a logical flow. Lev Kuleshov, a

Russian filmmaker, was the first to show the value of montage in the 1910s and 1920s. The Kuleshov effect is well-known; viewers interpret two consecutive pictures together more meaningfully than they do a single photo alone (for a lovely example, check out the Wikipedia page).

> ## Editing

• Move

G moves the selected strip(s) in its entirety. You may adjust the location of the strip in time by moving your mouse horizontally (left or right). To switch channels, move vertically (up or down). Snapping may be enabled or disabled by holding down Ctrl while dragging.

Moreover, you may use X to lock the direction in relation to time and Y to switch the channel of the strip.

Strips may be moved with a mouse by dragging them while holding down LMB. Dragging may only be used to move a single strip at this time.

• Start Frame Offset

You may choose the Start Frame Offset for that strip by clicking LMB on the left handle of the strip; you can also modify the start frame inside the strip by dragging it left or right by holding down the mouse button or by pressing G. The beginning frame of the strip is indicated by the frame number indication beneath it.

• End Frame Offset

The strip's End Frame may be chosen by clicking LMB on its right handle. The strip's finishing frame can then be changed by moving the mouse while holding down the mouse button (or by hitting G). The final frame of the strip is shown on the frame number label above it.

- **Extend or Move From Current Frame**

When you have multiple strips chosen, you may interact with the strips by hitting E. This can be used to extend (or reduce) time around the current frame; it works similarly to moving.

You can adjust the length of the strips at the current frame by transforming all chosen strip handles to the "mouse side" of the indicator.

- **Slip Strip Content**

You can reposition the contents in a strip with the Slip tool without having to move the strip itself.

- **Removing Gaps**

Regardless of whether the strips are selected or locked, remove the blank frames that appear in the present frame and the initial strip to the left.